REAWAKENING TO LIFE

new
June 03

OTHER BOOKS BY CARMEN RENEE BERRY

When Helping You is Hurting Me: Escaping the Messiah Trap (1988)

Loving Yourself as Your Neighbor: A Recovery Guide for Christians Escaping Burnout and Codependency (with Mark Lloyd Taylor) (1990)

How to Escape the Messiah Trap: A Workbook (1991)

Are You Having Fun Yet? How to Bring the Art of Play into Your Recovery (1992)

girlfriends: Invisible Bonds, Enduring Ties (with Tamara Traeder) (1995)

Who's to Blame? Escape the Victim Trap and Gain Personal Power in Your Relationships (with Mark W. Baker) (1996)

Coming Home to Your Body: 365 Simple Ways to Nourish Yourself Inside and Out (1996)

The girlfriends Keepsake Book: The Story of Our Friendship (with Tamara Traeder) (1996)

Is Your Body Trying to Tell You Something? Why It Is Wise to Listen to Your Body and How Massage and Body Work Can Help (1997)

girlfriends Talk About Men: Sharing Secrets for a Great Relationship (with Tamara Traeder) (1997)

girlfriends for Life: Friendships Worth Keeping Forever (with Tamara Traeder) (1998)

a girlfriends gift: Reflections on the Extraordinary Bonds of Friendship (with Tamara Traeder) (2000)

girlfriends get together: Food, Frolic, and Fun Times (with Tamara Traeder and Janet Hazen) (2001)

REAWAKENING TO LIFE

RENEWAL AFTER A HUSBAND'S DEATH

MARY ELLEN BERRY &
CARMEN RENEE BERRY

A Crossroad Carlisle Book
The Crossroad Publishing Company
New York • Berkeley

The Crossroad Publishing Company
481 Eighth Avenue, Suite 1550, New York, NY 10001

Cover Design: Mary Beth Salmon

Cover used by arrangement with PageMill Press,
Berkeley, California.

Printed in the United States of America

Library of Congress Cataloging-in-Publication Data

Berry, Mary Ellen, 1929–
    Reawakening to life : renewal after a husband's death / Mary Ellen Berry, Carmen Renee Berry.
        p.   cm.
    ISBN 0–8245–1978–7
    1. Widows –Religious life.   I. Berry, Carmen Renee.   II. Title.
BV4528 .B47 2001
248.8′66 –dc21

2001036542

1 2 3 4 5 6 7 8 9 10   08 07 06 05 04 03 02

Lovingly dedicated to the memory of
David A. Berry,
my best friend and husband
for forty-six years

And in memory of

Bob Adams	*Malcolm Meguiar*
Richard Briggs	*Roy Poliny*
Faye Copeland	*Woodie Prescott*
Gene Dipboye	*Oscar Reed*
Warren Anderson	*Chet Robinson*
Marv Dahlquist	*Emmanuel Hernandez*
Frank Graham	*Wes Sanner*
Clyde Gregory	*William Sedat*
John Huntington	*Lester Smith*
Earl Lee	*Joseph Ticchi*
Bill Little	*Norman Ulberg*
Rick Marse	*Harold Young*

One of the worst things in the whole world
has already happened to us
—we've lost our husbands—
and we're still here.
Not only have we survived;
we still find joy and meaning in life.
Like it or not, we're on the other side of it.

—ETHEL

Contents

ACKNOWLEDGMENTS

My favorite part of writing this book is the opportunity to thank the wonderful people who have contributed to its birth. I first want to thank the women who shared their stories of loss and renewal with me, so I could share them with you: Betty Adams, Faye Briggs, Annette Dipboye Coburn, Lurline Copeland, Maghy Anderson Davis, Helen Dahlquist, Gloria Graham, Jonnie Gregory, Ruth Huntington, Hazel Lee, Eileen Little, Sharon Hart Marse, Mabel Meguiar, Rita Poliny, Leslie Prescott, Grace Reed, Inez Robinson, Teresa Hernandez, Evelyn Sanner, Betty Sedat, Marvis Smith, Mary Ticcki, Janette Ulberg, and Ethel Young. I pray their candor and courage inspire you as much as they have me.

I want to thank those people who journeyed with me through my husband's illness and passing. Prior to David's accident, he was the teacher of the

Koinonia Christian Life Class at out church. During the four months he was in the hospital, members of the class visited almost daily and supported us with their love and prayers. Ivan Neufeld, in particular, seldom missed a day coming to boost David's morale. The steady supply of love and friendship gave me the strength I needed. I'd also like to thank the Del Rey Class, another Christian Life Class at our church, for their consistent prayer support, especially Inez Robinson, who called me every week to get an update and to provide me with an encouraging word. The women in my Tuesday morning Bible study, specifically in my small group led by Hazel Lee, gave me and continue to give me a safe place to talk about my grief, my struggles, and my triumphs.

I will be forever grateful to Lynn Barrington, who, from the night of the accident until David's death, helped us advocate for David's care as only a gal from Texas can. In addition, I thank those who tirelessly visited the hospital, stayed overnight when needed, researched information on the web, and helped out anyway they could — Marianne Croonquist, Cathy Smith, Bob Parsons, Pat Luehrs, Joel Miller, Rene Chansler, Tamara Traeder, Bob

Myers, Roy M. Carlisle, Miriam Smith, and Gail Walker.

Sumiyo and Sanji Kawakami, as close as family even though we live an ocean apart, have my deepest gratitude. When David had his accident, Sumiyo flew in from Tokyo to help Carmen and me with his care. Sanji joined her later, and they were both able to spend time with David before he passed away.

Reverend James and Dolly Goss were close friends to us for many years and were of special comfort presiding over David's burial and memorial services. I leaned on their strength during the dark days immediately following David's death and treasured Reverend Goss's words of faith and tribute. Special thanks to Dolly for her unique friendship and for singing one of David's favorite hymns at the service. In addition, I want to thank long-term friends Rene Chansler and Cynthia Bell for their musical contributions to the memorial service.

To my Japanese daughters, six of whom flew in from Japan to attend David's memorial service, I say, "Every year on the date of David's passing, a beautiful arrangement of flowers arrive at my door from Misako, Megumi, Mayumi, Junko, and Yuko.

They know they are always welcome because they are a part of my family."

My deep gratitude goes to Vera Gagner and the other hairstylists and manicurists at the House of Richard for their weekly attendance, not only to my appearance, but to my emotional needs as well. Their deep love and concern helped me cope with the loss of my husband and has been invaluable in helping me refocus my life.

In the practical matters of selling the family home and relocating, I want to thank Bob Myers and Dick Davis. Not only did they care for me as a real estate client, they cared for me as a person too. Starting over in my new home was made much easier due to my welcoming neighbors, Hugh and Phyllis Harris, Jack and Elma Decker, Margaret Herndon, Linda Lesh, and Betty Stradley. I'm grateful to my newest neighbors, Tim Lenderman and Bill Eckloff, who often come to my aid and take good care of me in so many ways.

Words cannot capture how important my long-term friends Wendell and Twylla Woods have been to me through this transition. Before David's passing, we were a foursome. While it is challenging for some couples to maintain a friendship with a "single" person, Wendell and Twylla have made sure our threesome has continued. We love the challenge of competing in our favorite card game, Hand and Foot. I also want to thank Evelyn Sanner for becoming my new buddy with whom I can grab a quick dinner or room with on our travels. She's always full of surprises and keeps me laughing.

The stress of losing David and moving to a new home left me physically exhausted. My physician, Dr. Phong Ngo, took the time to listen to me and to provide me with the best medical care. His genuine concern was more healing than the medication.

Even though I'll have to read this to them, I want to thank my faithful cat companions, Sailor and Sadie. To Sailor —thanks for all your "gifts" of rodents, and to Sadie —thanks for sitting in front of my computer and pestering me while I was working on this manuscript. These furry friends listen intently when I talk to them, my constant companions, providing never-ending entertainment.

I want to thank my daughter, Carmen, without whom this book would never have been completed. She's been the source of my strength through this entire process. We have cried together, laughed together, and now we have written together. This is my story, but she is an integral part of my journey.

A special thanks goes to Roy M. Carlisle for catching the vision of this book and having the stamina to see it through to completion. His editorial wisdom is unmatched, and I am honored to be one of "Roy's authors." Appreciation is extended to the entire staff of the Crossroad Publishing Company for their enthusiasm and support of the book.

CHAPTER ONE

WHEN THE SUN BREAKS THROUGH

Life is too precious to waste. When my husband died, I could have decided to go to bed and draw the shades and not ever see anybody. But I realized that there's a reason I'm still living and that I can't waste my life that way. So I got up and set off to find my new calling. —MARY

There was nothing unusual about that Wednesday morning when I awoke about the same time I usually did each day. I was in automatic mode as I descended the stairs to the kitchen to begin my morning routine. You see, I had lost the one I had shared my life with for the last forty-six years. During the months following my husband's accident, during his many surgeries, and after his death, a gray cloud of grief surrounded me. At times, that cloud seemed almost smothering. My world was an endless task of sorting through, saving, and shredding yellowed papers, filling brown paper bags with once-loved items to be donated to my favorite charity, and looking back through blurry eyes at what I'd lost. Yes, it was just another Wednesday, just another sepia-toned day to get through.

I walked into my kitchen and blinked my sleepy eyes. Everything around me seemed so different, so transformed. The room was vibrating with color. The brilliant sun shone through my white, lacy-curtained kitchen window in a spectrum of the most beautiful colors imaginable, which formed a rainbow as they danced across my kitchen floor. I felt a new awareness of everything around me. The kitchen stove seemed shinier, the white kitchen cabinets seemed whiter, even the very air I was breathing seemed as fresh as after a summer's rain. Just as Noah heard God's voice when he saw the first rainbow, it seemed that I heard God say to me, "Savor this season of your life. Refocus now on new opportunities. They are all around you, just waiting for you to tap into them. Don't waste your days and let these opportunities slip by."

In an instant, my life changed direction, as clearly and decisively as it had the moment I learned that my husband had died. I still missed him, but I realized that my life had not ended with his. I still loved him, but now it felt acceptable to laugh and grow and enjoy life, even without him. It was time to create a new life for myself—one in which I was not solely defined as a "widow," but as a woman who had experienced and survived one of life's greatest challenges.

The fact is, those of us who have lost our husbands have a choice — to live in the past or to embrace the present. Some women never move beyond their grief, defining themselves as half a couple for their remaining years. Others, however, build on the love they once had and re-create themselves as women larger than their losses. Some remarry, some don't. Some continue to live in the same house, comfortable with the familiar, while others move to new surroundings for a fresh start. Some invest more heavily in existing careers or volunteer activities, and still others set out to develop talents and dreams set aside because of previous commitments. Being forced to go through daily living without your partner can unleash forgotten talents or reveal unknown strengths.

When your husband dies, there are so many decisions to make and so many changes to adjust to. Where do you fit now that you're no longer part of a couple? How will you manage your finances alone? Who will carry your groceries into

I still loved him, but now it felt acceptable to laugh and grow and enjoy life, even without him. It was time to create a new life for myself — one in which I was not solely defined as a "widow," but as a woman who had experienced and survived one of life's greatest challenges. —MARY ELLEN

the house? The list goes on and on. Fortunately, there are answers to all of these questions. Out of the gray comes color, out of the challenges comes creativity, and out of the despair comes gratitude. What was so harsh as an ending will look more and more like a fresh beginning. It's possible to actually feel blessed to awaken to another day, blessed to awaken to this day.

I'm not the only woman who has had a dramatic reawakening experience after the loss of her husband. Rita, whose husband died suddenly after thirty-eight years of marriage, received her "welcome back to life" message at the mall. Only fifty-four when her husband died suddenly of a heart attack, Rita was taken completely off guard by his passing.

She told me, "Roy was one of the most loving, caring people I had ever met. He adored his family, and he loved his friends. We were always together. Even though he has been gone ten years, every now and then, our neighbors will say, 'It's hard to watch you without your shadow.' If I went shopping, he went with me. He even went with me to the beauty shop. Since he was only fifty-nine at the time of his death, I thought we had many more years together. He had taught school that day, in what seemed to be fine health. The next moment, a heart attack took him from me.

"Until it happens to you, you really can't imagine the feelings. A very good friend asked me, 'What does it feel like?' I can't describe it exactly, but it is as if someone takes a baseball bat and hits you as hard as they can in your stomach. You can't breathe, and you fear you'll never get a good breath again. You really walk around numb, like a zombie. I had always loved to read. But I no longer could concentrate and keep my mind on what I was trying to read. So I just put one foot in front of the other, one step at a time, and one day at a time.

"My turning point was such an unexpected event. I can remember the moment vividly — three years and three months after my husband died. One morning I went to the mall to shop for a new dress. I parked, got out of my car, and walked across the street to the sidewalk leading into the mall. When I stepped up on the sidewalk, I thought, 'Well, that's funny.' I looked down at the sidewalk, and then I walked a little further. Then I turned to look back at the spot where I had stood. If anyone was watching me, they probably thought I had lost my mind.

"Since my husband's death I had not, until that moment, felt the ground beneath my feet. My grief had been so very heavy. If it hadn't been for my faith and my family, I don't know what I would have done. I had been numb to the world around me, believing I was doing much better than I actually was.

"Feeling the earth once again beneath my feet gave me a sense of security, an energy of aliveness I hadn't felt for so long. I walked around the mall,

---

A very good friend asked me, "What does it feel like?"
I can't describe it exactly, but it is as if someone takes
a baseball bat and hits you as hard as they can in your
stomach. You can't breathe, and you fear you'll never
get a good breath again.   —RITA

---

so excited, wishing there was someone I could talk to who would understand! From that day forward, I've been back in touch with the world around me."

Of course, not every woman's reawakening is this dramatic. Many women I've spoken with experienced small awakenings that led to an awareness that their focus had shifted from merely getting through the pain of loss to the larger task of creating a new life. It can be difficult to know where grief ends and your new life begins.

Ethel, a retired college professor, told me, "I didn't know how to answer people who asked me how I was doing. I was confronted with this question so often. It was hard for me to know what the benchmarks were. How was I supposed to know how I was doing? I didn't know what I was supposed to be feeling exactly, or, specifically, what I should do in this situation because I had never experienced this before.

"All I knew was that when my husband died, I wanted to die too. My side of the family tends to live a long time. My mother lived to be 95, and my maternal grandmother lived to be 101. My paternal grandmother lived to be 91, so I saw my life stretching ahead of me with no meaning. I had lost my purpose and questioned whether my children or my grandchildren really needed me.

"Looking back, I can't say there was one overwhelming, defining moment when I felt that my life took that dramatic turn. There were many defining moments, many awakenings. My friends gave me all sorts of inspirational books and cards. Each one helped a little. One book promised that some morning you would wake up and the first thing you would think about would not be your husband and his death. You would think about the living room that needed to be vacuumed. I thought, 'That will never be.' Yet now I do wake up and have other things on my mind."

Living without our husbands can sap our will to live at all. However, in the face of our own mortality, we may discover a passion for life that we thought we'd lost. Ethel had such a realization when she got a bad report on a breast mammogram. She explained, "I had to go for an ultrasound and that wasn't definitive enough. So I had to go for a biopsy, and that frightened me very much. I wondered, 'What if I get a bad report?' I pictured the scenario where I'd be fighting breast cancer that could kill me. Much to my surprise, I realized that I wanted to live!"

Reconnecting to our personal life mission, a reason to live that extends beyond our marriage, can be the bridge from loss to a new awakening. Such was the case for Ruth. At the age of nineteen, she met and married a tall, lanky, handsome man who was just as happy and fun-loving as she was. After sixty years of a full and happy marriage, Ruth's world came to an abrupt halt. Quite unexpectedly, John suffered a massive heart attack and died.

Initially, Ruth appeared to handle the following days and weeks quite well. She arranged the funeral service, conducted the necessary business arrangements, and took care of the many facets of her daily life. Competent, chin up, determined, and independent, Ruth continued to live as if nothing had changed. After a few weeks, however, Ruth's veneer began to crack. But where could she go? Who could she talk to?

Her doctor was also a dear friend, so she decided to call for an appointment. When she entered the doctor's office, the nurse quickly noticed Ruth's sad, weary face. As the nurse questioned Ruth about her feelings and symptoms, Ruth explained that she

I'm so grateful the nurse gave me the chance to cry. That was my turning point. I felt I could finally move on with the necessary adjustments to life without my beloved John. —RUTH

could not sleep well, food did not appeal to her, and her mind seemed hazy. She felt so lonely.

The nurse knew Ruth very well and, taking Ruth in her arms, she said, "Ruth, you just need to cry. Go ahead and cry and get it all out." Ruth began to sob, and she cried and cried and cried. Until that time, she had not shed one tear. Her heart was breaking, but she had not been able to find any relief. Ruth told me, "I'm so grateful the nurse gave me the chance to cry. That was my turning point. I felt I could finally move on with the necessary adjustments to life without my beloved John."

Ruth is now eighty-eight years old. "I'm a happy gal to have survived eighty-eight years. I look forward to every new day. Now my job is to go every day to our senior center, where I take care of all the recent widows and widowers. I help put a smile back on their faces, the way the nurse put one back on mine."

We need other people during this process. No one can rebuild a life solely through her own power. Friends, family members, and even our children might be the source of that little nudge. With tears in her eyes, Teresa recalled how, after the sudden loss of her husband, that little nudge came to her through comforting words from her seventeen-year-old son. He gave her the hope and encouragement she needed to pick up the pieces of her devastated life, formulate a plan for the family, and move forward.

Teresa was in her thirties when she abruptly lost her thirty-seven-year-old husband, leaving her alone to raise four very young children and two teenagers. Teresa told me how after a hard day's work, her husband, Emmanuel, was relaxing in the family room watching TV. She said, "As he leaned forward to switch channels on the TV, he suddenly fell to the floor with a massive heart attack. Out of the blue, he was gone."

Teresa confided, "I was overwhelmed, trying to care for all the daily needs of the children. Little Roberto was only seven months old. Then there was Jason, aged two, Sylvia, aged four, Christina, aged five, Marie, fifteen, and David, seventeen. As some of the numbness began to wear off, many questions began to swim around in my head. What were we going to do? Emmanuel was always such a good father and provider. Where would the money come from? Where would we live? We couldn't afford to stay in the home we were now renting. There were so many decisions to be made."

Teresa and several of her family members had discussed a number of options, including going on welfare and moving into special housing. During the discussion, her oldest son, David, took her hand in his hand, looked her in the eye with unwavering conviction, and said, "Mom, we can make it." Those were the words that Teresa needed to hear. At that moment, she knew in her heart, no matter how tough the situation might be, the family would find the strength, faith, and courage to face whatever it would take to rebuild their lives. "We knew that rebuilding our lives would require a lot of financial creativity and ability to see options where none existed before."

The family pulled together. David and Marie worked after school to help support the family, while Teresa took care of the younger children during the day. When the teenagers returned each evening, Teresa had already fed and bathed the young ones and gotten them ready for bed. Teresa would then go to work, taking the graveyard shift, returning in the morning in time to get her children off to school. She said, "My new life was actually our new lives together as a family. I am so proud of my children. We all pulled together. They inspired me to go forward, when it would have been easier to give up."

Now adults, her children have held positions in a variety of capacities. David became a criminal investigator for Los Angeles County. One of her daughters is an office manager for the *Los Angeles Times*. Another son is a supervisor for a telecommunications firm, and yet another is a superintendent for a commercial construction company. Caroline, one of Teresa's daughters-in-law, told me, "From the moment I met Teresa, she has had the ability and charm to make everyone feel so welcomed and comfortable. She loves to prepare a meal for anyone who comes to her home. In fact, when her sons were growing up, their friends would come over to the house just to see Teresa. It didn't even matter if her sons were home. They just wanted to spend time with her."

In private moments, when we fear that there is no end to our grief, God's presence can comfort us like no one else. Janette told me, "I relied on God when my husband was alive, and I felt God with me after he was gone." Janette receives enormous comfort through a strong sense of God's presence and through memories of fifty years with her husband.

Smitten with Norm when she was merely fourteen, Janette told me, "I kept my age a secret for quite a while. After all, Norm was a much older man of twenty. When you're underage, those six years can seem extremely important!

"It didn't matter to me, however. From the moment I saw him I was hooked — we dated at church affairs and went for rides in his beautiful car, a blue 1937 Chrysler club-coupe. He spent three and a half years in the Air Force, and we were married just before my eighteenth birthday.

"I loved him always, it seems. We were never apart. When I had something to do, we did it, and when he had something to do, we did that together too. After he retired, we had thirteen wonderful years traveling all over the U.S. and to many foreign countries. We were both in fine health, so losing him was the last thing on my mind.

"One Tuesday morning, as on every Tuesday, Norm left to pick up groceries for a ministry at our church that provides food and clothing to people in need. He gave me a hug and a kiss as he left and said he'd be home early. Without a second thought, I went on with my day.

"Around noon the phone rang. A friend from the church told me to come over there right away. I drove to the church and was told that Norm had collapsed, most likely with a heart attack, and had been taken to a local hospital. A friend rode with me. Once we arrived, a nurse led me in where a doctor said, 'We did all we could.'

"It was such a shock to hear those words. I couldn't cry. I couldn't believe it. I simply walked into the room where he was, stood there for a moment, then leaned down and kissed him good-bye.

"My family came and some stayed for several days, which was a comfort. But you still have to go in and face going to bed alone. That first night I prayed, 'God, just help me get through this night.' And he did. The Lord was so close that night and has been every night since. I am so grateful for the fifty wonderful years that Norm and I had together."

Janette showed me pictures of a cruise that she, Norm, and their family of fifteen had taken six months before Norm died. She told me, "We went to celebrate our fiftieth anniversary. Little did we know that this would be our last year together. The cruise was such fun. I have so many memories. In fact, our last six months have a special glow to them as I look back on them now. Over Memorial Day, we visited one of our sons who commented about how happy we were and how much fun we seemed to be having together. A month later, Norm was in heaven. I live each day as it comes, drawing comfort from the sense of God's presence and love in my life, and in the gratitude of so many wonderful memories of life with my beloved husband."

After my own husband's death, I got a lot of comfort from the Lord's prayer in which Jesus teaches us to pray: "Thy kingdom come, Thy will be done on earth as it is in heaven." I wanted my husband to be restored to complete health, but I prayed for God's will to be done. I choose to believe that, as painful as it was for me, God's will included my husband's death. I don't understand it, but God's presence is powerfully real to me and, even through the valley of death, I trust him.

WHERE DO WE GO FROM HERE?

The women in this book illustrate that there is no one way to grieve, or one way to move forward in life. During my freshest grief, my friends gave me many books on death, dying, and grief. Quite frankly, I was in too much pain to read them. When I could finally focus my eyes on a book, well into the first year, no one gave me material on how to create a truly satisfying new life. I had moved beyond the most difficult grieving period, yet I had no idea what to do next. When I looked around, however, I saw many courageous women re-creating lives worth living. I decided to tell their stories and mine as well.

The important thing to remember is that in order to move forward, we all must be willing to let God reshape who we are and give us new purpose. There's no way around it. As women of faith, we know that we do not go through the valley of the shadow of death alone. God has promised us peace even in the midst of our grief.

As months pass and we mark that first anniversary, then the second, and third, and so on, many women invest the emotional energy that was used in their marriages into other relationships. These investments won't replace your husband — no one could. But from your new relationships, you'll eventually enjoy a sense of satisfaction and gratification, perhaps not identical to what you received from your marriage, but rewarding and meaningful just the same.

When I get up in the morning now, I still go to my kitchen for breakfast and begin the routines of my day, but I don't see those dancing rainbows on my floor. Oh, it is still a pretty, bright, and sunny place, but it is, after all, just a kitchen. I still have my moments when I keenly feel my loss, when I am sad and wish that my husband were here to share and enjoy something with me. But the memory of the colorful, dancing rainbow is mine to keep. Life *is* too precious to squander. So, as long as I'm alive, I choose to cherish and savor each fresh, new day.

REAWAKENINGS

- *Give yourself plenty of time to grieve.* No two women take exactly the same amount of time to reach that turning point between being part of a couple and starting a new life. For some it will be a few months. Others will find that it takes years to get to this new place.

- *Put one foot in front of the other, one step at a time, and one day at a time.* We don't need to feel pressured to move any faster than we

35

are moving or to have the slightest idea where we're going. Leave direction and timing to God and simply be willing to let God reshape who you are and give you new purpose.

     Expect good things. It may seem like you'll never be truly happy again, but trust me. You will be.

CHAPTER TWO

WHEN KEEPING THE FAITH DOESN'T KEEP HIM ALIVE

*I'd bring out the Bible and read, "If you ask any-
thing in my name you will have it. Would you
offer your child a stone?" But when I had asked,
when so many of our friends had asked for God
to heal Chet, it didn't happen. If felt like God had
indeed given me a stone.* —INEZ

My faith in God's continuing purpose for my life
has provided the foundation for living meaning-
fully. During periods of loneliness, I sense God's
presence, which eases my pain and reminds me
that I am loved. I don't know how I could have
gotten through this tremendous loss without my
relationship with God.

I must be honest, however, and acknowledge that
in times of crisis, faith can also be misunderstood

or misapplied, leaving us disappointed, confused, angry, and cut off from a vital source of comfort. Faith can be used as a way of running from reality rather than facing life and death squarely. When my husband passed away, I was unprepared to face my loss. I had more questions than answers. How could he be gone? I had been at the hospital every day, making sure he was well cared for. I wasn't ready for him to go. How could God be ready for him to go? All of our friends at church were praying for his recovery. Why hadn't God answered our prayers? How could I trust that same God to take care of me now that I was alone?

Many of the women I've spoken with have voiced similar feelings. Some ask, "Didn't God hear my prayers? Maybe I didn't have enough faith. Maybe there was something more I could do? Am I being punished? Why has God let me and my husband down?" These and other disconcerting thoughts can fill our minds.

HAVING FAITH OR FINDING FAULT?

Death is so final and painful that it's natural to place blame on someone — anyone. We can direct our anger at ourselves, the doctors, our husbands, and even God. We ask ourselves, "What could I have done differently?" "If I'd made different decisions that day, maybe he'd still be alive," or "Why did I miss the signs that seem so obvious to me now?"

Ethel fell into this way of thinking when her husband died from a heart attack. She recalled, "I felt a lot of guilt at first. I blamed myself. Could I have prevented his heart attack? If I'd fed him better? If I'd nagged him more about exercising? If I had insisted? I have a friend who said, 'I just march my husband to the doctor's office and tell him what's what.' I thought, 'Why didn't I do that?'

"After a while I shifted the blame to the doctor for not being attentive enough. He knew Harold was overweight, but he didn't push him hard enough to get in shape. Then I was angry at Harold for not taking better care of himself. I have moments of anger with him still, that he wasn't exercising enough or eating right. If he'd only listened to the doctor, he might still be with me. I went through various stages of fixing blame. It was especially difficult when I felt that God had let me down."

As Christians, our faith in God serves as an anchor in life's turbulent seas, a guiding star when we have lost our way. And yet during one of the most painful crises we could ever face, the God we turn to for comfort can seem to vanish, leaving us without our husbands and without a sustaining faith.

FAITH OR DENIAL?

Oddly enough, holding on to the belief that God will heal someone we love can keep us from facing the fact that, in some situations, God's timing is not ours. When we need to be saying "good-bye," we may feel we're being faithful by saying "hang on." Holding on to the belief that God will heal our husbands may actually rob us of the opportunity to say what still needs to be said before time runs out.

Such was the challenge that Margaret experienced when her husband was diagnosed with cancer. "He simply refused to talk about his illness, only about the fact that God was going to heal him. He was unwavering in his faith that he was going to get well.

40

"My husband was a strong-willed, creative man. I would often tease him by saying that whenever he walked into the room, the room was full. After being a minister for twenty years, he moved to the world of business and investments. When he found out he had cancer, he approached this challenge

Holding on to the belief that God will heal our husbands may actually rob us of the opportunity to say what still needs to be said before time runs out.
—MARY ELLEN

just as he would approach any other situation in his life. This man of great energy and determination searched for a cure, any cure. He followed the traditional route but also traveled to Mexico and to Canada to get nontraditional treatments. These special treatments extended his life for a few extra months, but did not lead to a permanent cure of his cancer.

"I think it was a combination of the way he viewed his faith and the impact of the strong drugs he was taking that caused him to withdraw from me and our children. The only people he seemed to respond to was a group of minister friends who came regularly to pray with him. None of us were allowed to discuss the possibility of his passing. To him, that signified a lack of faith, and he would not tolerate any doubt. Eventually, he went into himself, and the family never got to have that final good-bye. I've heard stories about great epiphanies when each family member gets to say something of meaning, or set things straight, or just say, 'I love you.' We didn't get to do that. He just went away emotionally and then he died."

Margaret's husband is like many men who meet challenges head on. When they are faced with a life-threatening illness, our husbands may try to control their destinies the way they tried to control everything else in their lives. Mix in a strong faith that God will provide healing, and without meaning to, our husbands may forbid their families to confront the possibility of death. If the men we love cannot acknowledge that their days are few, we are robbed of our chances to verbalize what we feel or discuss arrangements we need to make. When death finally comes, we may feel unfinished, still having so many words left to say. Without proper closure, there can be a literal aching of the heart that medication can't touch.

Margaret felt that pain. She not only lost her husband, but also the chance to share his last moments with him, having been shut out long before her husband passed away. Looking back, she told me, "I needed closure but didn't know how to get it. So I did the only thing I knew to do, and that was to cry out to God."

At the end of her long, tiring, work-filled days, Margaret sat at her husband's desk and cried her heart out. Then she turned to her Bible for the strength that she needed for the next day. "The Psalms were of great help and encouragement to me, giving me words to pray when I didn't know how to put my own feelings into words. Night after night, I ended my day at my husband's desk — to cry, to pray, to read, and to feel God's closeness. Eventually I realized that I was shedding a few less tears as the ache gradually receded. My sense of comfort increased, and slowly I said to God what I had wanted to say to my husband."

Margaret's family also helped her get the closure she needed — not only through tears but through laughter as well. Margaret told me, "My children and their spouses would often get together and tell hilarious tales of the many crazy misadventures my husband got himself into. We'd laugh until we cried, and then we'd cry until we laughed. The process helped us all digest the loss and make peace with his passing."

UNWILLING TO LO/E

Coming to terms with loss isn't easy for any of us. It seems to be especially challenging for take-charge people. Inez, still going strong in her eighties, is

I needed closure, but didn't know how to get it. So I did the only thing I knew to do, and that was to cry out to God. —MARGARET

this kind of woman. She has reached her goals in education, in business, and at her local church. If you want the job done, just ask Inez. Inez does not recognize the concept of "losing" —she's a winner. And yet, having fought to the very end to get her husband the very best care, Inez lost her battle to save her husband, Chet, from a fatal heart attack.

She told me, "We had gone to bed on a Friday night. Chet awakened with a horrible pain that he couldn't get rid of. He'd been diagnosed with a hiatal hernia, so he got up and took soda water to relieve it. When nothing worked, I took him to the emergency room at a nearby hospital. They admitted him for observation, and I went home certain he'd be back in a day or so. In fact, I even went ahead with a party we'd planned the next day. It never occurred to me that this would be serious.

"When he was still in the hospital on Sunday, I started getting worried. People came from our church and prayed for Chet's healing. When I left that night, I asked the nursing staff to call me if anything went wrong. I was assured they would. However, when I got there the next morning, the day nurse told me that he was very ill. She asked, 'The night shift didn't call you?' I told her no. Then she told me that Chet had had two major heart attacks during the night.

"We moved Chet to another hospital with more sophisticated cardiology services. I pressed the doctors about doing a bypass operation, but no decision was made. They kept running more tests. On Monday, they discovered blockages in his heart, and Chet went to surgery that evening.

"A large group of people from our church came and spent the night at the hospital. We prayed and prayed. One man told me, 'I had this vision that Chet's going to be healed.' I grabbed on to that with all my might.

"Initially, the surgery was going well, and they thought he'd be fine. But then they turned his heart over, and it was 60 percent gone in the back. We hadn't suspected he had heart trouble because Chet had never had chest pains or heavy pressure on his chest. All his pains were in his back. Now I know why.

"His heart stopped beating during the surgery so they put him on a heart machine. Things looked really bad. The nurse was pessimistic. She said, 'Mrs. Robinson, please don't get your hopes up.' The surgeon asked me, 'What do you want us to do if he goes into cardiac failure?' I asked him, 'What would you do if that was your father?' He said, 'I would let him go.' I said, 'Well, I won't let him go without a fight. Do everything that you can to save him.'

"My friends kept praying, and many encouraged me by saying, 'You've got to keep your faith up, Inez. You've got to keep your faith up.' And I did. I stayed at the hospital nearly round the clock. I'd come home between 4:00 and 5:00 A.M., take a shower, and go back down there. I didn't sleep in a bed for days. I was in a constant fight against death. They talked to me of the possibility that he might not ever leave his bed. I thought, 'That's all right. I can handle that. I know just what I'll do' — and made plans in my head about taking care of him at home. When he started improving on Wednesday, the nurse also felt optimistic and said, 'Well, maybe he'll make it after all.' So I was encouraged.

"But on Thursday morning I walked into ICU, and I looked at the monitor. I talked to him, but he never responded. I realized that there was nothing more I could do. Soon after Chet went into cardiac failure and every effort was made, but he didn't survive.

"When death comes, you can't fix it. You can't solve the problem. Even after my husband died, I was still fighting for his life. It took me a long time to realize that it really was over. It was so hard for me to believe that Chet was actually gone because I had so strongly believed that God would heal him. People had prayed.

"My church had been a place of comfort to me before Chet's passing. Now it was painful to be there. I'd go to class, and I'd hear these testimonies, 'God healed me here,' 'God healed me there,' and on and on. I'd get where I just couldn't stand to hear anyone else's positive stories. I kept asking God, 'But what about Chet? He was a great man. He was a great churchman. He was everything you'd want in a husband, a father, a grandfather, and a church member. Why didn't you heal him, of all people?' It made the loss all that much harder on me.

"I'd bring out the Bible and read, 'If you ask anything in my name you will have it. Would you offer your child a stone?' But when I had asked, when so many of our friends had asked for God to heal Chet, it didn't happen. If felt like God had indeed given me a stone.

"One thing that helped me during this time was that our pastor, who was also a close personal friend, didn't try to force a pat answer on me. One of my granddaughters was especially angry with God for Chet's passing. She and her friends had gone to the hospital specifically to pray for him so it was a terrible blow to her when he died. My son

When death comes you can't fix it. You can't solve the problem. Even after my husband died, I was still fighting for his life. It took me a long time to realize that it really was over. It was so hard for me to believe that Chet was actually gone because I had so strongly believed that God would heal him. —INEZ

went to our pastor and asked, 'How do I answer her? She's so angry.' The pastor said, 'I don't know. I'm angry too.'

"When I heard the story I smiled. It was more comforting to know that it was okay to be honest about how we felt than it was to pretend to have all the answers. The fact is, no one knows why God didn't heal Chet. All we know is that we prayed for it, and it didn't happen. I was angry about it, my family was angry about it, and, thank God, our pastor was angry too."

No longer comforted by her faith, Inez felt confused. But she had a reawakening one afternoon while listening to the tape of a sermon by Dr. Lloyd Oglevie, former pastor of the Hollywood Presbyterian Church and later chaplain to the United

The bottom line for me is that I am to follow Christ regardless of where the path takes me. I've let go of the feeling that I've been treated unjustly. I stopped feeling such burning anger, which allowed me to move on.

—INEZ

States Senate. Inez recalled, "He spoke on the passage where Jesus told Peter he would die a martyr's death. Peter, not thrilled at that news, looked over at John and said, 'What about him?' Jesus said, 'Well what's that to you? You follow me.' That really spoke to me. I am asked to follow, even if my life path isn't as easy as someone else's."

Even though it's been years since Chet's passing, Inez still doesn't know why God felt it was time to take him. She believes that other people pray, and God does grant healing to their loved ones.

Inez affirms resolutely, "The bottom line for me is that I am to follow Christ regardless of where the path takes me. I've let go of the feeling that I've been treated unjustly. I stopped feeling such burning anger, which allowed me to move on."

Inez discovered that sometimes we are asked to move on with our lives before we have all the answers. Life can be messy, and our faith doesn't always provide a simple answer for all of the variables.

BUT GOD PROMISED TO HEAL HIM

Another woman who felt certain that her husband would be healed was Faye, who was seventy when her husband died. She told me, "I have learned many things about myself, about our world, and about my God that are of great value to me. When Richard, at seventy-three, was hospitalized with hepatitis, I was reading in the Psalms, and suddenly my attention was focused on the verse, 'The Lord will sustain him on his sick bed and restore him from his bed of illness' (Psalms 41:3 NIV). I was not searching for a promise concerning Richard's well-being at the time. However, this scripture seemed to jump out at me. I was impressed that God was saying to me, 'Your husband will be healed.'

"Never in all my reading of the scripture had I experienced and claimed a promise so whole-heartedly. From that moment I chose to believe that my husband would be restored to me. My faith said, 'Richard would recover.' I told everyone about this promise — my church friends, my family, and even the doctors and nurses at the hospital, whether they were Christians or not. I was certain."

But day after day, Richard's condition worsened as complications developed. After he'd been in the hospital about a month, the doctor advised Faye to call their son, Howard, to come as soon as possible. Faye followed the doctor's orders, but she did not believe that Richard would die. She said, "That night, the nurse asked me if I needed someone to go home with me. I said, 'No.' I was strongly holding on to God's promise from Psalm 41:3. At that moment, I was experiencing God's sustaining grace, physically, mentally, and emotionally.

"Howard and his family arrived the next night. We had a great week together with Richard. It never entered our minds that this might be our last time with him before he went to heaven. During that week, Richard experienced God's peace as he prayed for God's will. Richard told us that the most difficult aspect at this time was relinquishing the dream of seeing his three grandchildren grow up. He seemed to be preparing for his own departure, but I *still* did not expect him to pass away.

"On Friday morning, I received a call from the hospital telling me that Richard had died at 6:00 A.M. I was stunned. It was impossible. What had happened? How could I have been so mistaken about my special promise that Richard would be restored to health? This promise had been the source of my strength during the past weeks. I had shared my promise with Richard's nurses and doctors. I had shared my promise with my family and friends. Now I was grieving, confused, and humiliated, all at the same time."

God did not choose to make manifest the verse that Faye had held on to with such stamina. "I called my son and told him how embarrassed I was — and how let down I felt by God. It was as if my whole life of faith built up to that moment of utter disappointment. Why had God let Richard die? How could I have been so off the mark? I had just lost my close companion, lover, and friend, plus I lost my spiritual bearings as well. I felt very, very alone."

Faye and her son had many conversations about faith, disappointment, and the infallibility of God. Faye acknowledged to me, "God hasn't given me answers to every one of my questions. I still do not know why God chose to take Richard from me at that moment. At the same time, I have felt God's undeniable presence. He has not forgotten me, nor do I believe he makes mistakes.

"Richard and I were inseparable. The years we walked together had intertwined Richard's life

I still do not know why God chose to take Richard from me at that moment. At the same time, I have felt God's undeniable presence. He has not forgotten me, nor do I believe he makes mistakes. —FAYE

with mine. Only God knew the pain I experienced. As I prayed and looked to God for a clear mind, he slowly brought peace to my heart.

"I do have the peace of God, which transcends all understanding, even though I still don't understand it all. His grace brings me all I need to fulfill his will for my life. I praise God for his sustaining grace and for my dear family and friends who surrounded me with their love and concern. I can say with the psalmist, 'But I trust in your unfailing love; my heart rejoices in your salvation. I will sing to the Lord, for he has been good to me' (Psalms 13:5–6 NIV)."

Did we want God to heal our husbands? Of course we did. And we prayed sincerely for it. But God did not fulfill our prayers the way we wanted. In spite of this tremendous disappointment, we must move on. The question is, will we move forward to a more mature faith or will we lose our faith in God altogether? Only you can answer that question for yourself.

REAWAKENINGS

↪ *It's okay to be angry with God, or to be confused or unsure of your faith.* Be honest about your feelings with God. God is strong enough to handle any emotion or question you have and will be there to help you through this experience.

∽ *Protect yourself from others who can't tolerate your feelings and doubts.* You will undoubtedly come into contact with people who are uncomfortable with your doubts and confusion. In response, you may be given simplistic, unhelpful advice or be made ashamed of how you feel. Don't pretend to have answers you don't really have. God honors honesty, and so will those around you who are spiritually mature. Don't spend time with people who aren't truly supportive and helpful.

∽ *Live in your faith and visit your doubts.* While it's understandable that we'd be angry and disappointed when our husbands pass away, we will suffer even more if we allow these feelings to dominate our thinking and decision making. Don't put your life and faith on hold because you don't have all the answers. Seek out competent, mature spiritual counsel and explore these questions, but don't take up residence in the dark land of doubt. We are asked to follow God, regardless of what life holds for us. God will give you comfort and insight as you walk in a maturing faith.

⤳ *Allow God's presence to comfort you.* The scriptures are full of prayers by people who were confused, angry, grieving, and overwhelmed. God gave us these prayers, I believe, to confirm to us that he knows how we feel and that there is much in this life we cannot fully understand. Open your Bible to the book of Psalms, for example, and you may find the words that capture exactly how you feel. Allow God's presence to comfort you.

CHAPTER THREE

WHO AM I WITHOUT HIM?

I can't tell you exactly when he wasn't the last thought on my mind at night or the first thought on my mind in the morning. But I gradually became reconciled to living without him.

—INEZ

"Honey, you are facing reality, aren't you?"

My blurry eyes focused on the concerned face of the nurse attending my husband. Reality? I wasn't sure what that was anymore. Nearly four months had passed since my husband, David, aged seventy-one, had tried to trim a large limb from a tree in our front yard. The limb had snapped, and I found him lying on the ground with serious cuts on his face. A neighbor ran up to help. I dashed for the phone. Soon, the paramedics appeared, and the next thing I knew a doctor was telling me that my husband had broken two vertebrae in his neck and both bones in his lower left leg. Many surgeries followed, while my daughter and I held doggedly to hopes for his full recovery. After three weeks in the hospital, David was moved to a hospital that specialized in rehabilitation therapy. After six weeks of therapy, we made preparations for him to come home. We were hopeful, even though he wasn't quite himself, but then after all he'd been through, who would be?

Our hopes dimmed abruptly once he was home. His physical wounds were mending, but his mind was confused. I was unable to care for him, even with nursing assistance and help from friends and family. Determined to keep him out of a nursing home, my daughter moved him to her home, where she, a part-time nurse, and I cared for him around the clock. David became more and more disoriented and unmanageable. Finally, we realized that he needed more care than we could give.

We moved him to a nursing home, where the staff was attentive and helpful. We began to adjust to the idea of long-term care in such a setting since it appeared that, though my husband had survived the accident physically, he'd never get well mentally. Then he had a stroke. And then another one. The nurse standing in front of me was trying to prepare me for a good-bye that I didn't want to give.

Early the next Saturday morning, exactly four months and one day after the accident, I received a call from the hospital. I was informed that David was slipping fast. I headed for the hospital.

Upon arriving at David's bedside, I sensed that he was trying to tell me something. I knew that he wanted to say good-bye. I kissed him and told him that I knew what he was trying to say. I told him that I loved him and that I understood it was time for him to go. He visibly relaxed.

Soon, friends and family gathered around his bed, held hands, and prayed. No one wanted the story to end this way, but we all released him as best we could. The nurses couldn't tell us how much longer he had — a few weeks, a few days. Once we let go, he was free to let go, and he passed quietly within a couple of hours.

Was I facing reality? Looking back, others may have seen that his death was imminent, but I wasn't ready for us to be separated yet. The last thing I remember of normal life was when I stuck my head out the front door and told David to finish up with that tree because it was time for us to leave for an appointment. Fifteen minutes later when I came out to the car, he was lying on the ground. I woke up that morning expecting an ordinary, forgettable day, not the last day that I'd have a coherent conversation with my husband of forty-six years, and certainly not the beginning of the end of life as I knew it.

READY OR NOT

No matter when or how you lose your husband, it's impossible to be completely ready. There's no practical way to rehearse for this tragedy, and who would want to? So ready or not, we plunge deep into a river of grief, and by the time we wash back to shore, gasping for air and grateful to find solid ground under our feet, our lives are changed forever. We may not want to be changed, but I believe that God intends that each of us allow this suffering to strengthen our faith and prepare us for the next phase of our lives.

Not all women see it that way. I've known some who adamantly resist any transformation after losing a husband. They keep their homes exactly as they were before their husbands died, inadvertently creating shrines of cuff links and power tools and dusty books as if life has stood still. And indeed, for these women, the goal is to act as if "it" never happened. If we have defined ourselves as Mrs. So-and-so, it's easy to cling to the past by becoming Mrs. So-and-so's widow. Rather than seeing ourselves as individuals in our own right, as women with many life experiences, which include surviving the death of our husbands, we may be tempted to define ourselves solely by our husbands—whether they are living or not.

But let's face it—none of us wants a new reality. We want the lives we created with our husbands. Unlike welcoming a new baby into our families or launching an exciting new career, this curve in the road is unwelcome and painful beyond words. It doesn't matter if you're young, expecting to spend the rest of your life with the man you love, or older with years of memories together, there's never a right time to lose your husband. As Jesus prayed passionately in the Garden of Gethsemane to "let this cup pass," we also resist drinking from such a bitter cup.

Evelyn and Wes met when they were in high school. They attended the same church and, even though they were not officially allowed to date, they always managed to spend time together at the

It doesn't matter if you're young, expecting to spend the rest of your life with the man you love, or older with years of memories together, there's never a right time to lose your husband. —MARY ELLEN

many church socials. After high school, they attended the same college. Evelyn was a junior in college when she and Wes, two years her senior, were married. Eventually they were blessed with a beautiful baby girl and a bright, healthy baby boy. Their lives were centered around their church, where Wes was a very active leader serving in many capacities. Evelyn, an accomplished pianist, was always in demand.

Even though they enjoyed many happy years together, Evelyn was not ready to lose her husband, Wes, when he was diagnosed with Lou Gehrig's disease at the age of seventy-five. She recalled, "This was a trying and difficult time for everyone. In addition to giving Wes the care he required day after day, I tried to cope with his imminent death. After months of struggling to accept the fact that my husband was growing weaker and weaker, I realized that I must let Wes go. I prayed one afternoon, sensing that God wanted me to relinquish Wes to his care. I relied daily on the verse, 'Be still and know that I am God' (Psalms 46:10 NIV). Finally, when I was able to let go, I experienced a peace I never thought was possible."

The act of "letting go" may sound like giving up, but it takes a great deal of courage to surrender to such a loss. Our husbands' time on this planet has ended. We, however, are alive, not as a leftover part of our husbands, but as women for whom God still has purpose. Paradoxically, when we are able to release our loved one to the care of his Maker, it is the start of our new beginning.

One woman who was confronted with redefining her purpose in life is Ethel, the retired college professor mentioned previously. Even though Ethel had a doctorate in education and a distinguished teaching career, she told me, "My identity was very much wrapped up in my husband. I felt that being

Harold's wife was my most important role and that my career was peripheral. Our marriage was the hub of my life, and all the other activities went out from the center of this hub.

"When Harold died suddenly from a heart attack, I felt like I was cut in half. I wasn't a whole person anymore. I was talking to a friend of mine, and I drew two circles for her — one being me and the other Harold. I said that our circles overlapped so much there was only one circle. She said, 'Ethel, you are still yourself. You have your own identity. Even though your circles overlapped, you still have your own circle.' That insight helped me a lot. It's been five years since Harold died, and I now experience myself as a whole person. But at the time, I couldn't imagine ever feeling 'right' again."

Sharon is another woman who survived feeling cut in half. Today she has a thriving therapy practice and is raising her two sons as a single parent. But five years ago, Sharon was mostly a stay-at-home mom of thirty-four when Rich, her thirty-six-year-old husband, was fatally injured in a car accident.

She told me, "On this particular March morning, I arrived as usual at my part-time job. Once at work, however, I felt very unsettled and restless. Unable to calm my mind and focus on my work, I finally told my boss that I felt I should go home. I got on the freeway, and about two exits from my house, the traffic was at a stop. Turning on the radio to check the traffic report, I heard that there had been an accident. They were bringing in an airlift helicopter to transport a victim to the hospital. I decided to get off the freeway.

"Unbeknownst to me, Rich was the accident victim mentioned on the radio report, but I did not connect my internal distress with a car accident reported by radio. Distracted, I got off the freeway, took care of some of my usual errands, and picked the boys up from school, telling myself this tense feeling was just in my head.

"Around 6:00 P.M. one of my husband's colleagues called and said Rich had not come to work. Worried, he came over, and we called all the surrounding hospitals to check whether anyone had been brought in. They all said no, except for one hospital, which said they had a John Doe there. They were completely unhelpful and wouldn't even tell me if the man was alive or not. I was told I'd have to come down and see for myself.

"My dad and brother-in-law drove down with me to check whether the John Doe was actually Rich. All the way down to the hospital, I thought about how upset Rich was going to be when he found out that I had gone down to the hospital to check on a John Doe. I thought, 'He's going to come home, and I'm down here doing this thing, and he's going to think it's crazy.'

"We got to the hospital and found Rich on life supports. Even though he had his wallet with plenty of ID, no one had called me. The doctor told me straight out that Rich wasn't going to make it. I asked him what was the percentage for his chances of recovery. The doctor said, 'If you need a percentage, he has a one percent chance to live.' I said, 'If he has a one percent chance, I'm going to hold on to that.' A picture of Rich and me in the future came to my mind — of us speaking at church or at a conference, putting a carton of one percent milk up on the podium and telling of our one percent miracle.

"I sat by Rich's side and prayed, 'God, if it's your plan to take Rich now, I'll accept it. But please do not let this be an act of the devil in our lives.' An overpowering sense of peace came over me at that moment. My father and brother-in-law felt it too. I knew then that God was taking Rich home. I thought of the hymn, 'It Is Well with My Soul.' The Lord assured me that Rich's accident did not take him by surprise and that I was not alone. I held on to that with all my might. Rich never woke up. His injuries were too severe, and he passed away around 2:00 A.M. the next morning."

FINDING NEW PURPOSE

The moment Rich died, Sharon entered a new season in her life. At such a time, all that any of us can experience is the sadness and the grief. But it is possible to look back later and see that in the process of grieving we also lay the foundation for our new lives. While breaking the painful news to others, planning the memorial service, managing our finances on our own, and simply getting through the day, we learn how to cope without our husbands. Each step in the mourning process is one step closer to reawakening to a different way of being in the world.

Looking back, Sharon told me, "It has been five years since Rich's death, and so much has changed.

It Is Well with My Soul

When peace like a river attendeth my way,
When sorrow like sea billows roll;
Whatever my lot, Thou has taught me to say,
"It is well, it is well with my soul."

Though Satan should buffet, tho' trials should
   come,
Let this blest assurance control,
That Christ hath regarded my helpless estate,
And hath shed His own blood for my soul.

My sin—oh, the bliss of this glorious thought!
My sin—not in part, but the whole—
Is nailed to His cross and I bear it no more,
Praise the Lord, Praise the Lord, O my soul!

And, Lord, hast the day when the faith shall
   be sight,
The clouds be rolled back as a scroll,
The trump shall resound and the Lord shall
   descend,
"Even so"—it is well with my soul.

—H. G. STAFFORD AND P. P. BLISS

My boys were only ten and twelve. Now they're growing into men themselves. Five years ago, I saw myself as a wife, mother, and homemaker. Now I am the sole financial support for my family. I earned a doctorate in psychology and see myself as a professional woman in addition to my role as mother. And, being single now, I am finally dating again and exploring whether or not love is possible for me a second time. But one thing hasn't changed, and that's who God is. I am sure God still has my life in his hands."

Sharon distinctly remembers her reawakening — the moment God spoke to her about her future and the assurance that her life's purpose had not died with Rich's death. Sharon recalled this moment. "My father wanted me to attend a special occasion where he was being honored as he retired as dean from a seminary. It took every ounce of strength I had to even get dressed, let alone go out and be sociable. Like a lump, I sat there listening to the many wonderful tributes to my father, with my mind still in that hazy, I-can't-believe-this-has-actually-happened fog.

"Through the blur, I felt the Lord tell me that even though Rich had died, I still had a purpose to fulfill. It was a turning point for me—a starting point, actually. I let go of the sense of incompleteness since Rich's death, accepting that neither I nor our boys had the chance to look him in the eye and say good-bye. I realized at that dinner that God had begun a good work in me, and he'd complete it. At the time I didn't know what that plan might be, but I felt comforted that I was a part of something larger than my sorrow. There was a bigger picture, and I couldn't see either the beginning or the end, but I had a viable part to play."

Holding on to the belief that God has a purpose for us, with or without our husbands, is essential for re-creating a meaningful life, especially during those times when we may feel like we're groping in the dark, lacking a voice from heaven or a bolt of lightning to lead the way. Sometimes we feel God has forgotten us. Even those women whose faith has had decades to strengthen and mature can feel destabilized and uncertain during this process.

One woman I spoke with had been a missionary and minister's wife for her entire adult life. No stranger to coping with difficult situations, Hazel was the oldest of six children, and her mother was an ordained minister. Her mother was often away from home, and Hazel was left with the major tasks of caring for her younger siblings.

Hazel excelled in all her classes in school and graduated as salutatorian from college. Before she graduated, she met the man she would marry. Hazel fell in love with Earl the first moment she

Holding on to the belief that God has a purpose for us, with or without our husbands, is essential for re-creating a meaningful life, especially during those times when we may feel like we're groping in the dark, lacking a voice from heaven or a bolt of lightning to lead the way. —MARY ELLEN

saw him walking across the college campus. She told me, "Without my realizing it, Earl became the center of my life. I was shy and serious, and Earl was extroverted and optimistic. We complemented each other well."

The first years of their marriage took them to several cities in the Northeast to pastor congregations. Then they served as missionaries in India for fourteen years. Hazel raised a family of three children and was active in the ministry. She said, "When we returned to the States, I was forty-two. Rather than pursue a career of my own in teaching, I decided to fulfill the traditional role as minister's wife to the large church that my husband pastored. At the time I felt completely rewarded."

The responsibilities of a pastor's wife are many. Hazel blossomed into a respected elder. She authored or coauthored five books. She played an active part in developing ministries for the women of the church. Hazel and Earl traveled internationally and throughout most of the United States, speaking together at conferences and seminars. They were a team.

In 1999 Earl and Hazel were vacationing on a cruise when Earl became faint — the beginning of an illness that took his life six months later. Hazel said, "I have to admit I was surprised that his passing had such an impact on me—physically, emotionally, even spiritually. Here I had lived in India for fourteen years, bearing three children and raising a family, learning the language and wearing many hats. Plus our son was one of the hostages captured in Iran in 1979 and held captive for 444 days. He was released on January 1, 1981, which was also my birthday—truly the greatest birthday present I have ever received. Until his release, the pain in my heart was constant. Through it all," she told me, "my faith held firm. I thought nothing could be worse than this.

"But Earl's death rattled me in ways I never expected. I was not nearly as prepared or as strong as I thought I would be. During his relatively short illness, I didn't try to imagine life without him. I didn't think I needed to prepare myself because I thought I could handle anything. But when he died, I had a true identity crisis. I felt very weak physically and lost a lot of weight. I kept asking myself, 'Who am I on my own, without Earl?' It was so very, very painful not to know the answer to that question."

Reestablishing her new life and identity has happened in small steps. One turning point was when Hazel accepted that life was never going back to where it was before. "Realizing that my life had profoundly changed was where I had to begin. I didn't have Earl to rely on, but as I made decisions about my new life, I discovered that I could trust my choices.

"You can't continue to look back over your shoulder," Hazel told me with a hearty laugh. "I feel like a pilgrim, finding my way in this life at the ripe old age of eighty-three. I find it rather strange. My life was definitely tucked under Earl's. We had many wonderful years of marriage, working closely together. I loved every minute of life with that tall, lanky New Englander who laughed so freely. He made me love life. He was a one-dimensional thinker, a typical New Englander. Nothing about my life has ever been simple. I have hurdles to mount. I am waiting for the time when I feel strong enough to once again attend the church where we spent the nineteen happiest years of our life. I am still not ready for that hurdle. Maybe I'm just protecting myself because I have been so raw emotionally."

Hazel isn't in a hurry, nor should she be. She is still finding out new things about herself each day, exploring different avenues of service. "I believe that God has purpose for my life, even though right now I'm in a bit of a holding pattern, exploring possibilities. It's a process, and I'm moving forward. That feels wonderful."

In order to rebuild our lives, we have to reconsider previous self-definitions. The role that fit when we were married no longer does. Being still, sensing God's sustaining presence, and believing that God has continued purpose for our lives will give us new courage to redefine ourselves. It is always difficult in the beginning, but we will discover

Being still, sensing God's sustaining presence, and believing that God has purpose for our lives will give us new courage to redefine ourselves. —MARY ELLEN

that the essence of our true selves rests in no fixed label, but in the capacity to experience life in a different dimension now.

Our purpose in life is indelibly linked to our personal sense of identity. As Therese Rando writes, "You must become accustomed to the absence of an integral part of your life, someone who has contributed to your world and life being what it is. You will have to learn to be in the world without the person who was a partner with you in the unique relationship the two of you had, a special relationship that helped make you be you."* Who

---

*Therese A. Rando, *How to Go On Living When Someone You Love Dies* (New York: Bantam Books, 1991), 229.

we believe ourselves to be —wives, mothers, ministers, counselors, and Christians —influences where we invest our creativity and passion.

Who are we without our husbands? While many things change when our husbands die, we continue to be beloved children of God. God has purpose for your continued time on earth. Discovering this new purpose will probably not come to you in an instant, although you may have distinct moments of clarity. Most of us find our way, step by step, day by day, as God awakens us to a new calling.

REAWAKENINGS

⮑ *Hold on to the belief that God has a purpose for you.* Your life did not begin when you married your husband, nor does it end when he dies. God is mindful of you and has something special for you every moment of your life.

⮑ *Work toward accepting that your life has changed and will never be the same.* While it's natural for us to hold on to the cherished past with our husbands, the fact remains that our lives will never be exactly like they were. What a painful realization! But once we accept it, we can stop resisting and start cooperating with God's new purpose for our lives.

↬ *Don't expect to be perfect through this process.* Allow yourself time to learn how to cope with life in new ways. You didn't know instantly how to be a wife. You won't know instantly how to be a widow, either. It's okay to make mistakes. Just view them as learning experiences. If you were wise enough to marry a man you miss this much, you must be a woman who can make good choices.

↬ *Don't push yourself.* There's no reason to go back to those old familiar places or spend time with people who, without meaning to, trigger painful memories, bouts of loneliness, or raw emotion. As you become more comfortable with your new adventures, the pain associated with certain locations or relationships will soften, and eventually they will serve as comforting reminders of the love you enjoyed.

Chapter Four

All in the Family

One of the first steps I took was to deliberately get up, get dressed, put on my earrings, and try to look good for the sake of my children. These simple tasks would leave me exhausted, and after I got my sons off to school, I'd have to take a nap.

—SHARON

Along with redefining ourselves after our husbands passed away, most of us find that our relationships with other family members are also altered. We aren't in this grieving and rebuilding process alone—we are in it as a family.

Everyone intimately related to our late husbands must confront their own loss, each dealing with their pain in individual ways. We may find enormous strength in helping our children cope with their loss. Sometimes it's hard to know who is the so-called older and wiser one when out of our children and grandchildren's mouths come insight and wisdom. We may experience a role reversal with our adult children, as they look after us more than we look after them. Holiday gatherings, family traditions, and anniversary dates serve as poignant reminders that a beloved husband, father, son, or brother is no longer where he's "supposed" to be. New traditions, reflecting our new family structure, take shape and before long become mainstays in our new lives.

REBUILDING YOUR LIFE FOR THE SAKE OF YOUR CHILDREN

Every woman who has rebuilt her life after her husband's death has had moments when she consciously chose life over death, determination over defeat. We've all had mornings when getting out of bed required more energy than we could muster, days in which our only goal was to endure until sundown, nights so dark and long we feared that morning would never arrive. Each one of us has had to find a strength of purpose to go on.

Something or someone served as motivation for us to put one foot in front of the other and move forward. Those who are mothers, especially those whose children were young when their husbands died, told me that their primary motivation for surviving was to help their children overcome this tremendous tragedy.

Sharon's sons were ten and twelve when their father died. "The most difficult thing I had to do was to tell my boys that their father had died. My father and I broke the news to them, and they cried non-stop. They just wept until they could no longer cry, until there were no tears left. Finally, we looked at each other and knew we had to go on.

"My family and friends actively attended to our needs, especially on those days that I was so numb I could hardly boil water. One day I was driving with my father, and I turned and asked him if these feelings would ever go away. I was wracked with fear, feeling that I had to be on high alert or something terrible would happen. Being a man of great wisdom, my father assured me that in time my extreme feelings would subside, but that I would go through a process. I asked him how long it would take. He told me that if there were no complications, approximately a year, perhaps even longer. I thought, 'Then for my sake and for my boys, I need to do whatever it takes to heal.' The strength I received from my family and friends I passed on to my sons.

"I felt God's presence and that no matter what had happened, God was still in control. I realized that nothing enters my life not ordained by the hand of God, and I was impressed with the fact that there is still life to live because I am in it. My life

My sons have many fond memories of their dad, and I have intentionally kept those memories alive. I've reinforced the fact that their father gave them what they needed to grow up and be well-balanced men.

—SHARON

was not over. I began to heal, and beyond healing there was comfort. It would have been very easy to fold up in my sorrow.

"One of the first steps I took was to deliberately get up, get dressed, put on my earrings, and try to look good for the sake of my children. These simple tasks would leave me exhausted, and after I got my sons off to school, I'd have to take a nap. When they came home, I tried to present myself well. I wanted to model for them a determination to go on living."

As Sharon's sons have grown, they've asked different questions about their father and have voiced their concerns about growing up without a dad. Sharon said, "I've been aware that there were those places only a father can fill. Consequently, I have worked very hard to encourage the boys' masculinity. I wanted them to develop as normally as possible even though they'd lost their father.

"My sons have many fond memories of their dad, and I have intentionally kept those memories alive. I've reinforced the fact that their father gave them what they needed to grow up and be well-balanced men. Today, my older son is a senior in high school and my younger son is a sophomore. I think the death of their father helped them to develop a keener sense of life and its brevity. They have had to grapple with the meaning of death. They seem to be a little more introspective than other boys their ages."

Sharon's devotion to her sons motivated her to move forward when she was tempted to give up. I interviewed another woman who had a similar experience raising her daughter after two serious family losses. Helen told me, "The first tragedy struck our home when our daughters, ages five and seven, were in a terrible car accident with my brother-in-law. Our five-year-old was seriously injured and died five days later.

"We had not fully recovered from this loss when Marv became very ill with cancer. He was minister of music and minister to youth at our church and, because of his illness, he had to resign. Fortunately, I had already started working and was able to keep the bills paid and our needs met during his illness.

"Two-and-a-half years after Marv's diagnosis, he passed away at only thirty-eight. I drew my strength from my faith in the Lord, the support we received from a very dedicated pastor, and my devotion to Janice, my remaining daughter. Even though I was devastated, I realized that my daughter had suffered great loss at an early age. My focus shifted from myself to creating and maintaining a happy home for my daughter, not a simple task under the circumstances. My daily devotions and much prayer were essential."

Helen created a home where Janice could enjoy life, in spite of the losses. Helen told me, "I tried to fill Janice's life with joy by scheduling trips. We enjoyed our adventures together. And I entertained her friends as often as possible. I wanted our home to be a place where laughter came easily and fun was commonplace. I tried to keep a light spirit, and made sure that we had fun things to do along with our daily responsibilities. After Janice's graduation from high school, I was able to put her through college, as I knew her father would have wanted.

"My daughter was a great comfort to me during my grief and a source of enormous joy as we made a new life together. I take no credit for the way we came through those dark years, but I do give much credit to the wonderful pastors, church friends, and a few friends from my work who stood by us. Most of all to my Heavenly Father.

"Janice is now married to a wonderful Christian man, who like her, is a very talented musician. Together, they are creating a loving Christian home for their children. I think her father would be very proud of her. I know I am."

We can re-create our families, though not according to our original ideal. The new configuration can be just as full of love and as capable of laughter and happiness. Father and husband will always

I wanted our home to be a place where laughter came easily and fun was commonplace. I tried to keep a light spirit, and made sure that we had fun things to do along with our daily responsibilities. —HELEN

be missed, but stability, a sense of hope, a fund of support, and a life of accomplishment need not be sacrificed. God always has purpose for the living and brings us together in new, albeit challenging ways.

FROM THE MOUTHS OF BABES

As we invest ourselves in helping our children grieve and then in rebuilding their lives, we discover that our lives are also being rebuilt. It's hard to know exactly who's helping whom through this process. Ethel told me that she has received tremendous encouragement and spiritual wisdom from her daughters and her grandchildren. "My family has given me great joy. Their affirmation and love have been incredible. I'm a grandmother of twins, a boy and a girl, who are almost thirteen, and I don't know where I'd be now without them.

"I really must admit that I had a crisis of faith when my husband, Harold, died. I was shaken to my core and doubted heaven and whether I'd actually see Harold again. It bothered me that the Bible said that there's no marriage and no giving in marriage in heaven. I thought, 'If I'm not married to Harold, if I'm not with him in heaven, then I don't want to be there.'

"One day when my grandson, Andrew, was about eleven, he asked me, 'Gramma, is heaven really real, or is it just a fairy tale?' They called Harold Buppy when they were toddlers and the name stuck. Not having enough faith of my own to answer that question, I said, 'Well, Buppy thought heaven was a real place because he said this world is not fair, and he believed there had to be a place where everything was fair.' My grandson and I talked about children who suffer and how that's not fair. I said, 'Buppy believed there was a place where the crooked was made straight and the rough places were made smooth. That's heaven, Andrew.' And that satisfied him.

"Not long after that conversation, I went out to watch Andrew play baseball. He played a particularly good game that day. Afterward I said, 'Oh, I wish Buppy could have seen you play today.' He looked me in the eye and said matter-of-factly, 'Oh, he did. He and Gramma Hazel (Harold's mother) always watch me play. They even help me catch the ball.' His certainty about spiritual things helped my faith. I held on to Harold's and Andrew's trust in God."

Ethel also receives encouragement from her granddaughter, Natalie, who is quite a pianist. Ethel recalled, "At Christmas each year, Natalie plays her piano recital in her teacher's beautiful living room in San Clemente, California. During the first concert after Harold died, I missed him terribly and wished he could be by my side to enjoy this precious moment. Afterward I said, 'Oh, Natalie, I wish Buppy could have heard you play.' Like her brother, she felt very connected to her grandfather. She said, 'Oh, Buppy heard me play.

God made it more beautiful by the time the music got to heaven.'

"I didn't know what to say. Something inside of me knew that what she said was true. Later, I was saying Natalie's prayers with her one night, and she whispered, "Buppy's right here. Can you feel him? He's right here.' The faith of my grandchildren children has really given me courage."

HEY, WHO'S THE PARENT HERE?

Those of us whose children were adults when our husbands passed away may have found ourselves in a role reversal. After losing her father, my daughter, Carmen, has become quite protective, to the point that she keeps track of my every move. One night, perhaps a year after David died, I went over to a friend's house to have dinner and play some card games. Time got away from me and before I knew it, it was eleven o'clock. When I didn't answer my phone, Carmen came by my house to check up on me. Not finding me home, she started calling my friends.

When she got me on the line, she said the very words I used to say to her when she was a teenager.

"I don't care how late you stay out, just make sure I know where you are!" After she calmed down, we had a good laugh at the role reversal.

I'm not the only woman who has had to deal with overly protective adult children. Kathryn told me, "I can still look after myself. But my kids check in on me every night at 10:00 P.M. I feel like they

I've finally accepted the fact that, as a family, we must go through this ritual — the nightly phone call to see if I'm okay. To be more practical, you'd think they'd call in the morning. It's more likely for people to die sometime after midnight. But I don't think that's what this is really about. They just want to know that I'm home. They need a sense of where I am. —KATHRYN

treat me as if I were some wild teenager. They say, 'Are you in for the night? Are you all tucked in your bed?' I say, 'Oh, yes, I'm all taken care of.'

"Normally I answer the phone by giving my name. But when the phone rings at ten, I know it's them calling. I answer the phone with 'Hellllooww!' And I'll hear, 'Hellllooww!' right back. And if I don't answer the phone, they send out a posse. One night

I woke up with my kids standing at the foot of my bed. I had gone to bed early and slept so soundly that I didn't hear the phone ring. They got worried and drove up to look for me. They came right in and were standing by my bed staring at me when I opened my eyes and said, 'What are you doing up here?' They shrugged and said, 'When you didn't answer your phone, we came to see what was going on.'

"You'd think they'd have enough to do with raising their own kids and managing their jobs and lives. But I've finally accepted the fact that, as a family, we must go through this ritual — the nightly phone call to see if I'm okay. To be more practical, you'd think they'd call in the morning. It's more likely for people to die sometime after midnight. But I don't think that's what this is really about. They just want to know that I'm home. They need a sense of where I am."

Families change when they lose a member, and until it happens to you, it's impossible to predict just how relationships will shake out and rearrange themselves. Parents help children. Children help parents. Parents must listen to the words they uttered years ago as their adult children take on a more protective role. Grandchildren and grandparents provide comfort and faith to one another. While no one would choose to go through this experience, we may find that our familial relationships deepen and prosper in ways we never expected. The newly rearranged family can feel intensified intimacy.

TRANSFORM YOUR TRADITIONS

Family traditions that developed during the years you and your husband were together, such as holidays, birthdays, and anniversaries, may now serve as a painful reminder of your loss. The sight of red roses like those he gave you each Valentine's Day or the smell of hamburgers on an outdoor grill like those he used to cook each Fourth of July can trigger fresh bouts of sadness. How do you get through Christmas or Thanksgiving with one less seat at the table? Can you ever enjoy these traditions again?

During the sixty-seven years that Mabel and Malcolm knew each other, they developed many traditions. Mabel told me, "When we met in August of 1932, it was love at first sight! Malcolm had just turned seventeen and I was only fifteen when we met, but two years later we were married in the same church that we both attended for the next sixty-five years."

Malcolm truly adored Mabel, and from the early days of their courtship he always took advantage of the holidays to show his deep commitment. One evening when Mabel and an older sister were at home, the doorbell rang. Mabel told me, "We were taught to never open the door at night unless we knew who was there. My sister asked who was there, but no one answered. She asked again and again, and still there was no answer. Finally, my sister shouted that whoever was there had better answer or she was going to call the police. Still no answer. We were really frightened.

"My sister peeked out the window and saw Malcolm hiding in the bushes. Only then did she open the door and in disgust, she asked, 'Malcolm, just what do you think you are doing?' It was the first of May, and he had left a beautiful May Day basket at the door. He had rung the bell and hid, trying to be romantic." The romance never faded over the next sixty-five years. Each May first, Malcolm gave Mabel a beautiful May Day basket to let her know she was the love of his life.

I observed Mabel after she had lost her constant companion of so many years, unsure of how she was going to adjust to life without Malcolm. They had been inseparable, and I didn't know if she would be able to move forward as a widow creating a new life and new identity for herself.

As the weeks and months passed, I saw a sparkle returning to her grieving eyes. Mabel talked to me about her grief. She said, "I cried, screamed, and even jumped up and down as my heart was breaking. How could I go on? But throughout our lives, Malcolm and I relied on our trust in God. We were no strangers to his intervention during our years together. I firmly believe that God opened my eyes to my many blessings. I was reminded of a wonderful and happy marriage of sixty-five years, a caring church, a very close family that was always there for me, a great heritage, and a world of Christian friends.

"One challenge for me was dealing with those special days that Malcolm and I had celebrated together for so long. As the first Valentine's Day approached, I felt so alone. How could I go through this special day without Malcolm? I wanted to crawl under my bed and hide there all day. I knew

I couldn't spend the day alone, and I believe God gave me the idea of inviting two of my special friends, who had also lost their spouses, out to dinner. I discovered that they too were dreading spending this day alone, and they were delighted to accept my invitation. We shared a magnificent dinner and a lovely evening together.

"But God wasn't finished helping me through that day. Soon after I returned home from dinner, the doorbell rang. I opened the door and there stood a beautiful Asian girl, holding a Valentine's Day box of See's candy. She introduced herself as my new neighbor. I asked her to come in, and we talked for almost two hours. When asked what prompted her to visit she said, 'I don't really know. I simply had a strong feeling that I should come.' I knew why she was there. God had sent her to deliver a Valentine's Day reminder that I was loved."

Mabel repeated the Valentine's Day dinner again this year, adding another recently widowed friend to the group. She has decided to continue the traditional dinner, adding friends who are grieving. The traditions that she shared with Malcolm live on, transformed.

Mabel said, "If I have any advice to give grieving widows, I would say, 'You are not alone in your sorrow. Others are hurting too. Do something for someone else. If you make someone happy, pleasure and happiness will return to you. Accept invitations joyfully.'

"I've learned that even though there is a great void in my life, I can't change it. What I can't change, I must accept with God's grace."

The experiment that Carmen and I tried the first Christmas after David died turned out to be what I would term a "successful failure." Christmas had always been a big celebration in our home for the three of us. Neither Carmen nor I looked forward to going through the same motions with one-third of the family missing. We knew we must begin to establish some new traditions for just the two of us. Having always stayed at home for the holidays, we decided that we would travel each Christmas to a new location and enjoy a variety of cultures and celebrations.

In the early fall, we began to search for the right place to celebrate our first traveling Christmas. Immediately, a good friend suggested Williamsburg, Virginia. We collected materials on all the special

Christmas dinners and activities that took place there. It seemed almost too perfect. How wonderful it would be to be surrounded with the early traditional decorations, the beautiful old carols, and

If I have any advice to give grieving widows, I would say, "You are not alone in your sorrow. Others are hurting too. Do something for someone else. If you make someone happy, pleasure and happiness will return to you."
                                                        —MABEL

the lavish tables of foods so elegantly served! All the reservations were soon made, and we no longer dreaded celebrating that first Christmas without David.

Our excitement grew as we boarded the plane for Williamsburg. We could hardly wait to be surrounded by all the sights and sounds we had read about in all the brochures. In anticipation of colder weather, we were prepared with heavy winter coats, gloves, and scarves. To our amazement, when we arrived, the sun was shining and the temperature was delightful. We even shed our heavy clothing. As we were waiting for transportation to our hotel in Williamsburg, we were told that a winter storm was going to hit later in the evening. We were thrilled to think that we were going to have the added bonus of Williamsburg under a blanket of freshly fallen snow. What a perfect, if not magical, setting for establishing our new Christmas tradition.

After arriving at our hotel, we quickly unpacked, anxious not to waste a minute exploring this quaint little town. The wind had begun to blow a little harder, and it was getting colder by the minute. By the time we returned to our hotel, the cold wind and snow was stinging our faces. The cold had grown so penetrating that our heavy coats, gloves, and scarves were beginning to feel quite inadequate.

Our sleep was disturbed all night with the wind howling and the cracking sound of ice-covered limbs falling from trees surrounding the hotel. In the morning, we had to trade our dreams of a winter wonderland of snow for ice-coated sidewalks, trees, buildings, and highways. Out the window we could see that the ground was covered with broken tree limbs. Entire trees had cracked in half under the weight of the ice. Every few minutes, another limb would crash to the ground.

As we were standing at the window, the lights went out. The storm had brought so much ice to the area that there was a widespread electrical outage over a large portion of the state. The hotel and the whole town of Williamsburg lacked electricity. Maybe the early settlers of Williamsburg had known what winter would be like without electricity, but it is certain that my daughter and I were not prepared. Nor were the hotel employees!

Our Christmas dreams met the stark reality of no light, no heat, and no hot water for bathing. Even worse, the hotel was ill-equipped for such a situation, offering us only green glow sticks and a few candles but no holders. Carmen made makeshift candleholders out of our drinking glasses. The lavish, mouthwatering Christmas Eve dinner we'd expected became cold cuts, salads, and cold drinks. The restaurant couldn't even boil water for tea or coffee. The candlelight could have been romantic, but the dining room was so cold that we could only sit and shiver.

After dinner, we slipped and slid back to our hotel room, which was as cold as it was outside.

We slept Christmas Eve night clad in every piece of clothing we could find, huddled in one bed so we could double our blankets. I honestly thought we might freeze to death, being unaccustomed to this kind of weather. In the morning we packed our bags and carefully carried them over the slick frozen sidewalks — one eye on the ground to avoid falling and the other watching overhead for ice-laden branches still crashing to the ground. We begged a taxi to take us to the nearest airport and got back to Southern California as the sun set on Christmas day.

Did we begin the new tradition we had planned and dreamed of? No (and we'll never go back to Williamsburg, even in the heat of summer). Did we have a Christmas we'll never forget? That we did! It was so awful that we started laughing — and laughed and laughed and laughed all the way back home. Did we have time to be sad? Did we have time to think about how we used to celebrate Christmas? No, we were busy surviving the challenges of the moment. While I don't recommend revising your traditions this way, I must say that it worked for us!

Three Christmases have come and gone since David's passing. After the Williamsburg debacle,

Carmen and I have decided home is the best place for the holidays. The second Christmas, I cooked dinner for other widows and their daughters. Being with others experiencing a similar situation helped normalize Christmas without David.

Last year we celebrated at Carmen's place, with a houseful of our mutual friends. We had a ball — laughing, filling each other's stockings with little goodies, entertaining the cats with Christmas ribbon, and eating lots of chocolate. We even started a new tradition for lunch — serving Traditional Christmas Tacos instead of the usual turkey and ham. I think we've found just the right mixture of the new and the old, refreshing and comforting elements for our holiday celebration.

You'll want to keep some traditions close to the way you've "always done it." Other celebrations will serve you better with changes and modifications, and some traditions are best discontinued. Some women have started brand new traditions and explored alternative ways to celebrate important days. Allow yourself to experiment. And to the best of your ability, keep hold of your sense of humor. That's the best tradition of all.

REAWAKENING*S*

↪ *Model how to rebuild a life for your children.* Your children and grandchildren will watch you cope with life's challenges. They will learn from you how to start anew.

↪ *Keep fond memories of your husband alive.* Even though your children no longer have their father in the flesh, they still have a father in memory and spirit. You can reinforce their self-esteem and respect for their father if you recall his positive characteristics and your children's love for him.

↪ *Make it okay to be happy.* Many of us feel guilty when we feel happiness after our spouses die. In order for our children to grow into healthy, competent adults, however, they need plenty of laughter and joy in their lives. If it's okay for you to be happy, they will reembrace joy in their own hearts.

↪ *Accept support from your children.* Some of the wisest truths come from the mouths of children. Listen and allow them to comfort and encourage you. And it's okay if your children

102

fuss over you more now. They've experienced the loss of one parent, so they may be a bit more protective than before.

↬ *Transform traditions.* Invite new people into old traditions. Experiment and try new things. If one idea doesn't work, try another until you reach the point where traditions help you remember the good times. Feel free to discard or ignore any prior tradition that doesn't contribute to your new life.

↬ *Take comfort in memories.* When the memories of your husband bring you comfort instead of intense sadness, know that you're healing. Accept the joy of these memories.

CHAPTER FIVE

WHAT DO YOU MEAN, WHERE ARE THE PAPERS?

We knew that rebuilding our lives would require a lot of financial creativity and ability to see options where none existed before.   —TERESA

MONEY — WHO WANTS TO TALK ABOUT THAT AT A TIME LIKE THIS?

Along with the emotional challenges of losing your husband, your entire financial picture can change in an instant. Since discussing the possibility of death can be unpleasant, some couples cope by pretending it will never happen. When it does happen, a woman can discover that her financial situation will be quite different from what she expected. Recreating a stable financial base may turn out to be one of the most significant parts of building your new life.

Betty had no idea that she and her husband, Bob, were in such financial trouble. Having devoted herself to raising her three sons, Betty left all the financial decisions to Bob. Over the years he invested his energy into providing the family with lovely, beautifully furnished homes. Betty was happy to have Bob write the checks, pay the bills, and set up a family budget. As long as Bob was alive, the arrangement worked well.

When Bob was diagnosed with cancer in his early fifties, all effort went into his treatment. Neither Betty nor Bob wanted to discuss the possibility that he might die, and Betty found the topic of money crass and unsupportive. "I assumed so many things that didn't turn out to be true. Since Bob had taken care of the family financially while our sons were growing up and going off to college, I assumed that he would make arrangements for us in the event of his death. He didn't. I assumed that since there always seemed to be money for what we needed, we had a strong financial base. We didn't. And I assumed that, when the time came, I'd know how to manage financially. I didn't. I had a lot to learn.

"In fact, the day he died I found our bank records in his files, and we had nothing in savings, no life insurance, and only a small pension for me to live on. I was stunned. I actually had to borrow money to bury him."

Betty's sons, grown with families of their own, pitched in to help her in those early days. Her only assets were the condo that she and Bob were buying

I that assumed that he would make arrangements for us in the event of his death. He didn't. I assumed that since there always seemed to be money for what we needed, we had a strong financial base. We didn't. And I assumed that, when the time came, I'd know how to manage financially. I didn't. I had a lot to learn

—BETTY

but did not yet own outright. Fortunately, Betty receives a monthly pension, and she is learning to manage money by herself.

Betty may have been left with next to nothing, but at least she didn't find herself in substantial debt. Margaret was not so fortunate. When her husband died, she discovered that she was responsible for repaying nearly three million dollars to investors and the IRS.

Margaret explained, "Warren was a big man — outgoing and outspoken. He was optimistic and charming and entertained thoughts and dreams of the magnificent. All this energy and vitality sometimes got Warren into areas in which he lacked expertise.

"For example, he put together an investment deal in the 1980s, when gold was up to about eight hundred dollars per ounce. The prospect of mining for gold captivated him, so he found investors for his new business venture and bought all the necessary equipment. He bought trucks and dredges and all sorts of supplies needed to search for gold. Crews were hired to work a number of mines, inside and outside of the States. I told him that all this scared me, but he wouldn't listen to anyone who tried to pour cold water on any of his dreams."

Unfortunately for Margaret, Warren was much better at living in fantasy than coping with details, such as paying income tax or providing dividends to investors. "After his death, I was left with all the income tax returns to file, all the bank statements to reconcile, all the mountains of bookkeeping work to straighten out. I worked full time, and then every night I'd come home and face the pile of papers.

"Furthermore, the IRS came and demanded I verify that Warren's mining business had been on the up-and-up. Doubtless they thought it was some kind of scam. Since the price of gold was so high at that time, there were many such scams going on. Warren may have been unrealistic, but he genuinely thought he was going to strike it rich. I knew he hadn't knowingly cheated anyone, so I eventually found the documentation to prove that he had truly invested the investors' money and that he had a legitimate, albeit poorly run, business."

After three years of hard work, five garage sales, and the aid of a skillful attorney, Margaret began to get her nose above water. She settled with the IRS and the investors and was finally able to call herself debt free. When asked how her faith had sustained her, she replied that she had felt an unusual closeness to God. The verse "For your Maker is your husband, the Lord Almighty is his name, the Holy One of Israel is your Redeemer: he is called the God of all the earth" (Isaiah 54:5 NIV) gave Margaret the strength to accept whatever the outcome might be. The support of her three attentive daughters helped keep her going when she wanted to wave a white flag. Margaret is a true survivor. Most women would have found her situation much too difficult to manage, but she met her challenges head on.

Rebuilding your life often requires financial creativity, which means developing the ability to see options where none existed before. Such was the

For your Maker is your husband, the Lord Almighty is his name, the Holy One of Israel is your Redeemer: he is called the God of all the earth. —ISAIAH 54:5 NIV

case with Teresa and her family of six children. Their story is one of ingenious creativity. Everyone was ready to pitch in and help, but what could they do? Teresa began to look at the few options available to her. Questions began to swim in and out of her mind. Where would the money come from to raise six children? They couldn't afford the nice home they were renting. Where would they live? How would they keep food on the table? They needed money to pay the rent and buy groceries, shoes, and clothes for the children.

The family was destitute except for their one prized possession — a 1956 sparkling green and white Pontiac. Teresa recalled, "Emanuel and I had scrimped and saved in order to replace the run-down, faded blue 1945 Ford we'd been driving. We drove proudly around town to show all our neighbors our newly acquired possession, the 'car of our dreams.' Little did anyone know just what an important role that almost-new car would play in our lives."

As some of the numbness began to wear off, Teresa began to think about where she might turn for some financial help. Her mind immediately turned to the Pontiac. Emmanuel had taken out an insurance policy on the car that included a death benefit, never dreaming of actually having to use it. Now, the finance company holding the pink slip would pay the balance owed on the car, making it entirely hers.

Teresa sold the car for two thousand dollars — a sum with much more buying power in the 1950s than it has today. She used the money as a down payment on a partially completed house with a small guesthouse in the back. Teresa squeezed her large family into the tiny guesthouse and went to work on finishing the front house. When it was ready, Teresa rented out the larger house in the front to bring in desperately needed income. Quite the entrepreneur!

While some women are unprepared to make financial decisions, others I spoke with were used to making financial decisions. Experience has demonstrated that planning ahead, however distasteful, gives a woman significant comfort during the process of starting anew. In the early years of our marriage, my husband had managed our combined incomes, paid the bills, and handled the taxes. In the last years of his life, however, he seemed to grow weary of these tasks and one by one, I took them over for him. I didn't realize at the time how I was being prepared to manage my own finances. By the time David passed away, I was fully involved in all aspects of our assets. While being solely responsible for myself financially was stressful, I was spared the anxiety that some women face who are unaccustomed to managing money.

A best-case scenario was described to me by Inez: "As far as the business part, it was no problem at all." Inez had been her husband's business partner and continued to manage their finances after they retired. She recalled, "We had set up our trust

---

I didn't realize at the time how I was being prepared to manage my own finances. By the time David passed away, I was fully involved in all aspects of our finances. —MARY ELLEN

---

not long before my husband passed away. We'd purchased our burial places at the Mountain View Mausoleum, so that part was not difficult. I kept track of everything anyway.

"Before Chet retired, and while we were in the contracting business, I took care of all financial matters with engineers, attorneys, the city, the state, and the sales. Chet's job was to see that everything was built, and my job was to keep track of the money. I knew exactly what we had and where it was, so the decisions of what to do financially weren't a problem. I'm so grateful that I didn't have the added burden of financial stress or confusion. In that regard, I moved right on."

The women who have the financial base to rebuild their lives quickly are those who have planned ahead and have educated themselves about family finances. If you are one of these women, you can feel proud of yourself and grateful to God and your late husband for the security you currently enjoy. If you are confronted with financial hardship, take courage and inspiration from the many others who have been in your shoes. Don't be afraid to ask for help and to draw strength and creative suggestions from your friends and family. God may provide for your financial needs in unexpected ways.

REAWAKENINGS

↪ *Don't waste time with "what ifs" when it comes to money.* If you and your husband set up a retirement plan, it was probably before today's financial changes and challenges. No matter what state you find yourself in financially, you are now in a phase of life where you need to manage your money on your own. It's unproductive to spend time regretting what you didn't do or what you thought you had.

↜ *Become a financial student.* If there are aspects to finances that you never learned, now's the time to become a wiser investor and money manager. Read books, take seminars, and talk to friends and family. There's a wealth of information available.

↜ *Think creatively about your finances.* If you find yourself in financial stress, don't fret. Instead think creatively. Solving the problem may turn out to be a source of enjoyment and a sense of accomplishment.

Chapter Six

Re-creating Home

The most private parts of our lives are disrupted when our husbands die. There's no one in bed beside us snoring at night, no one sitting in his favorite chair, no one cluttering up the garage with new bargains from the thrift store. —MARY

Immediately following our husbands' deaths, our homes remind us of the life that we used to have. You sip your morning coffee looking out the back window at the large tree that provides welcome shade each summer. You remember how your husband planted that tree as a sapling years ago. Absentmindedly you run your hand across the nick in the kitchen chair left that time when he sat down with his keys in his back pocket. There's his favorite chair in the den, the piano on which he would play "your song" each wedding anniversary, the shelf he was installing in the laundry room but never finished; his picture still sitting on your bedside table. Do these memories help us or haunt us as we rebuild our daily routines and living spaces? Is it better to stay close to these reminders or to move to a new location and start fresh?

No one can say what will work best for you. But of one thing I am sure — rebuilding our lives requires us to re-create our homes. During the painful task of sorting through my husband's belongings, deciding what to keep, toss out, or donate, I discovered that I could transform my living space from a source of pain to a refuge of comfort. As I rearranged the furniture to better suit my new projects, the past and present were integrated into a fresh and vibrant whole. In the process of deciding to sell my home or stay put, I set the stage for my future. Little by little, one small awakening after another, my home reflected more of the present and less of the past, including memories of my husband but making room for life on my own.

Some women feel most comfortable living in the home they once shared with their husbands. Inez and Chet built the house they lived in for over three decades, and Inez had no interest in leaving. She said, "I decided to go ahead and live in my house and to invest myself in the church and friends I've loved for so long. If I should change residences, I would never have the same peace of mind I have here. I suppose having lived in one place for forty-four years I may get a little too careless. I've even forgotten to lock the door from time to time."

Smiling mischievously, Inez said, "The front doors are handmade leaded glass, so I've thought about making a big sign: IF YOU PLAN TO ROB THIS HOUSE PLEASE USE THE BACK DOOR. I don't want those

---

Rebuilding our lives requires us to re-create our homes.
—MARY ELLEN

---

front doors ruined. I work from the theory that if someone really wanted in there's no keeping them out. No reason to worry myself at all. I'm so familiar with the noises and the quirks of this place that it's home for me, with or without Chet."

This is not to say that Inez merrily skips through her day unaware of the many reminders of her beloved. "Chet died right in the middle of adding a bathroom to our home. The two-by-fours were up, but the roof wasn't on yet. Nothing was finished. Chet had been the contractor, so I decided to do it myself.

"I'll admit that I hated the whole process. The addition is finished, but quite frankly I hate that room. I've wondered if the strain of that project contributed to his death. I don't think I'll ever use that bathroom, but completing it brought some closure to my grief. It was the first part of our home that I finished by myself. Everything else we had worked on together."

Making changes in the home you once shared with your husband transforms your living space, little by little, into *your* home rather than *our* home. You my not enjoy making these changes, but eventually these alterations form a comfortable backdrop to life as it is here and now.

While many of us don't face life with the same earthy practicality as Inez, feeling safe in our homes is a significant aspect of adjusting to living on our own. In contrast to Inez, I felt vulnerable and frightened in the home I had shared with David for over thirty-five years. The house seemed too large and dark when I entered it alone, even in the middle of the day. At night I jumped at each creak and noise, and I felt small in our king-sized bed. From the first night that David was in the hospital until I moved in with my daughter a couple of weeks after his death, that house never again felt like home.

As long as David was alive, living forty minutes away from my daughter, Carmen, seemed fine. However, those forty minutes seemed like forever

Making changes in the home you once shared with your husband transforms your living space, little by little, into YOUR home rather than OUR home.
—MARY ELLEN

when I was frightened or lonely. So within a year, I sold my home and purchased a two-bedroom condo a couple of blocks away from her — close enough so I felt safe yet far enough for us both to live our own lives. I'm less than two miles from my church now, close to my closest friends and to ample activities. Moving was the best way for me to re-create my life.

As you're contemplating what living situation best suits you, remember that you have time to ponder such a weighty decision. What might fit you the first year or two after your husband's passing may grow uncomfortable in the following years. Faye stayed in her home for three years after her husband, Richard, died. She told me, "I never had any thought of leaving the house that was our home for the past forty years, in which we shared so many wonderful memories. Each room was filled with the treasures we had accumulated over the years.

"Before Richard passed away, our son, daughter-in-law, and three grandchildren moved to California in order for our son to accept a new ministerial position. Richard and I helped them search for their new home, which turned out to have the cutest small cottage in the backyard. At the time, we joked about what a great grandparents' cottage it would be.

"Little did I know at the time that this cozy cottage would become my home. About three years after Richard passed away, my son and family asked me to live with them. I was ready by then to let go of the house that I'd lived in so long. My daughter-in-law had taken a teaching job, and I could be a great help to them if I moved to California. I sold

About three years after Richard passed away, my son and family asked me to live with them. I was ready by then to let go of the house that I'd lived in so long.

—FAYE

my home and distributed all the family treasures to other family members and friends. I really didn't need them anymore. I have never missed them.

"What a blessing to be needed by my grand-children. I receive so much satisfaction by being a part of their lives, and there is no other role I would rather fill in this time of my life. God is so good."

FACING HIS GARAGE

Whether the decision is to move or stay put, we all have to face the difficult question, "What am I to do with his belongings?" For many of us, our husbands housed most of their treasures in the garage.

My husband's garage was one of the biggest challenges I faced after he passed away. I have to admit that, in the thirty-three years we lived in that house, we never parked our car in the garage. My husband took it over immediately as "his space" and filled it to the brim.

First, he built shelving all around the room, with a spacious workbench along the back wall. After filling those areas to capacity, he built more shelving in front of the previous shelving. Like a labyrinth, the shelves wound around themselves until every square inch was stacked and packed. When he passed away, there was so much stuff in the garage that we couldn't walk more than two feet into the side door. Opening the front garage door was impossible, for it had long been blocked shut. Not only did we have to sort through, discard, and find homes for all these items, we also had layers and layers of shelving to tear down. I was adamant that my future would not include a garage packed wall-to-wall, floor-to-ceiling, with stuff "we might need someday." Until all the belongings were sorted through and the garage was cleaned out, I knew I'd be living in the past.

Not every widow has to face the garage challenge. But those of us who were married to pack rats, collectors, garage sale entrepreneurs (call them what you may), know about the hours of sorting, boxing, shredding, and driving to the thrift store donation bin. We're a special breed of women, whose new lives can be marked when the last article is removed and the garage floor is finally swept clean.

Margaret, another garage survivor, told me about her discoveries in her husband's garage. Margaret gasped, "The garage was unreal. In the middle of the garage, buried underneath a wide assortment of items, my husband had a 1948 Hudson. When all the stuff on top of the car was pulled away, we found that he had used the car as a storage space. Stuff was jammed inside the car from bottom to top. Around the garage were all of his tools, a workbench, and many things I didn't even know we had. I even unearthed a new microwave oven, which I now have in my kitchen. At least I found one thing that I wanted to keep.

"Besides the garage, the twelve hundred square feet of closet space in our house was also jammed. The attic was full. The basement was full. We lived in the same place for thirty-three years and that meant plenty of time to fill every nook and cranny with 'stuff.' I donated over a hundred shirts to our church for the young children to use as smocks when they painted. They are still using those shirts today, five years later."

REDECORATING YOUR LIFE

Lurline loves to rise with the sun. She spends hours in her kitchen, carefully preparing pies, cakes, and other delicacies for her friends and family. Whenever her husband, Faye, sold a home to a new family through his real estate business, he would come home and notify Lurline of the date the new family would be moving in. That was her signal to put together another of her home-cooked meals for the new homeowners. Faye figured that the family would be too busy and too tired to prepare food. That tradition became one of Lurline's contributions to their business.

As Faye's retirement date approached, they excitedly made plans to renovate and redecorate their home, inside and out. This was the home that she and Faye had built together years ago, the home where the whole family gathered every holiday, the home that the grandchildren loved. Unfortunately, before any of their many plans could be realized, Faye suffered a heart attack.

As Lurline began to recover from the initial shock of her husband's unexpected death, she thought about the plans that they had made together. She knew that to accomplish everything would require much thought, time, and energy. As the months rolled by, Lurline systematically tackled job after job, and her list of Must Do Today items began to shrink.

Each Friday is "hair day" for Lurline and me, and each week at the beauty shop, I got my usual briefing of the past week's activities. First, she had the house tented for a thorough fumigation. Then, she made many trips to the paint store for the paint chips to consider. The swimming pool, the place of so many Fourth of July picnics, needed a new resurface job. Lurline confided, "I've made a few changes in the house that Faye may not have liked. For instance,

I never really liked the dark wood paneling in the family room, but Faye couldn't see painting real wood. Well, it got the coat of paint that I always wanted. I must admit that I enjoyed doing it my way. And then there was the big taxidermy fish that Faye had caught on his favorite fishing trip and had proudly displayed in the living room. I moved the fish to the wall of the family room." She grinned, "I don't think he would mind too much. After all, I could have stored it in the garage."

No matter how much work it was to follow through with the alterations, Lurline had no thought of moving from the home in which she and Faye had shared so many wonderful memories over the years. The changes Lurline made to her home did not remove Faye's memory — rather they integrated it into her life as it is today. And she even admits to having a little fun getting to decorate strictly to her own tastes. Perhaps our husbands would think that we tossed out valuable treasures or picked colors they could never have lived with. But they had their say, and now we can change things solely to our own liking.

No one answer is right for everyone. Some women feel more at home in the house they shared with their late husbands; others feel oddly estranged from familiar surroundings and need to relocate to start fresh. Take time to examine a variety of arrangements until you find what will work best for you. You deserve to have a home that provides safety, comfort, and the opportunity to embrace a new way of living.

REAWAKENINGS

- *Give yourself time to decide where to live.* You need to decide whether you should stay in your current residence or move to a new locale. Some women are comforted by the familiar, and others need fresh surroundings to launch this new phase of life. Give yourself ample time to sort this out for yourself.

- *Be open to creative living arrangements.* You may discover that your ideal living situation is something you've never thought of before: a cottage in the back of a friend's home, a shared apartment with a girlfriend, or your own condo overlooking the sea. Open yourself to new options.

∽ *Let the process of going through your husband's belongings help you heal.* Sorting through the items your husband left behind can symbolize your emotional process, a tangible way to grieve and regroup. Letting go can be terribly painful, but as you do you make room for a positive future.

∽ *Only keep what you want.* Some things you'll never want to part with because of their meaning to you. But don't keep certain belongings out of a sense of obligation. Holding a garage sale or donating to your favorite charity can make use of items that you no longer need.

∽ *Enjoy making your own decorating decisions.* You miss HIM terribly, not that elk head over the mantle or his brown plaid couch in the family room. Now's your opportunity to decorate your living space exactly how you've imagined, without any negotiating or compromise.

CHAPTER SEVEN

SOMEONE STILL NEEDS ME

My daughter said to me, "Mom, I know your dream was that you and Dad would go through life together and that you would die in bed holding hands with each other. But that's not realistic. That's not the way life happens." At that moment I stopped asking, "Why me?" —ETHEL

I've not met one woman in my interviews who wanted to travel through the pain of losing her husband. In fact, many shared with me the various ways they tried to avoid feeling anything at all. God created us with an innate drive to survive, which includes a natural resistance to pain. Ever grab the handle of a hot pan? We all have, and without hesitation, we set it back down—quickly! No need to sit around and discuss your options. Ouch! It hurts. Get rid of this pain!

When our husbands died, our reactions were the same. Ouch! It hurts! Get rid of this pain! But unlike a burn from a hot pan, the only way to get rid of the emotional pain of loss is to feel it, express it, and let God go with us to the other side of it. The journey through loss will transform us into the women who continue living life to its fullest, the way God intends.

Since we women have a history of caretaking, it's easy to postpone our grief by throwing ourselves into the care of others. Rita told me, "I barely had time to realize my husband was gone when a close friend of mine was diagnosed with cancer. She lived up in the high desert, about an hour and a half from where I live, and without a second thought, I committed myself to her care. I went up every weekend to do what needed to be done. Taking care of her gave me purpose and focus, but it also masked my emotions. I thought I was doing so well with my husband's death. But then my girlfriend died, and both losses hit me at once.

"With her death, I stopped running. I finally let the sadness and loneliness wash over me. When the waves of grief subsided, I felt stronger, more flexible. Grief can change you for the better, even though I'll never stop missing my husband or my dear friend."

I am not implying by sharing this story that to successfully deal with the loss of your husband you shouldn't get involved with helping others. To the contrary, we heal and create new goals in the context of our ongoing relationships, often in our church communities. But we need to ask ourselves, "Is this relationship a way to participate in my grief journey or a way to avoid that journey?" Often, the answer is a little of both.

One woman I interviewed felt that her healing came from the process of helping others like herself. Betty told me, "After Bob's death, my prayer became, 'Lord, show me a way to make my life count. Show me a way to be useful in your kingdom.' I was in so much pain, but I knew that I had to find a new purpose, a different focus than being Bob's wife and the mother of my children. Our three boys were grown and married with families of their own. No one really needed me, and I didn't know where I fit in or where I might serve."

Without Betty's knowledge, her pastor had been observing Betty after Bob's death. When he felt it was time, he approached Betty and asked if she would direct a ministry in the church. She recalled, "The church had a grief recovery program called, 'Grief Share' — a thirteen-week program that met once a week. I was delighted, as it was a wonderful way for me to comfort others who had lost their

After Bob's death, my prayer became, "Lord, show me a way to make my life count. Show me a way to be useful in your kingdom." I was in so much pain, but I knew that I had to find a new purpose, a different focus than being Bob's wife and the mother of my children.

—BETTY

spouses. Being in those gatherings helped me cope with my own situation more effectively. God had surely heard and answered my prayer.

"I attended the training necessary for the demanding task of directing a ministry for people between the ages of thirty and ninety who were grieving over the loss of their spouses. As I meet weekly with the members involved in this program, I also progressed in handling my own loss. The one requirement to lead this program is that you have to know what you are talking about. You can't learn it in a class. You can't learn it from a friend who has experienced the loss of her spouse. You have to know it from your own experience."

I agree wholeheartedly with Betty. It's extremely hard to help someone who has lost a spouse if you've never experienced a similar loss. Before my husband died, I had no idea what my friends were going through when they lost their mates. In all sincerity I'd say, "Oh, how terrible," or "What a tragedy," or something similar. But until it happens to you, you cannot truly sense the depth of grief, the ache of loss, and the loneliness of nights that follow the death of your husband. But this experience makes us uniquely qualified to help others going through the same loss.

In her late eighties, Ruth lives each day with purpose, a sense of service, and a wide grin. But life was not always full of fun and laughter for Ruth and her husband, John. Their oldest son suffered a heart attack and died when in his early fifties. The following year, Ruth lost John, also from a heart attack. Ruth had a very difficult time when John died. She learned firsthand what it takes to grieve a tremendous loss and find new purpose in life.

Can you guess who is always called to assist when someone loses a spouse at the Senior Center? You are right if you guessed Ruth. She told me, "I sit with the man or woman who has just lost their spouse and say, 'If you want to cry, I'll cry with you. If you want to be quiet, I'll be quiet with you. When you want to talk, I'll listen.' So many of us have a hard time expressing how we feel — especially with tears. I tell them the reason they have tears is to cry." Ruth smiled, "It's cheaper than buying eyewash."

Ruth has approached her physical problems with the same pluckiness She's endured surgeries, injuries suffered from falling, eye problems, and some of the inevitable difficulties related to growing old gracefully. "It's okay to feel sad for yourself," Ruth informed me. "So cry when you need to, but then get up. There are others to think about who need comfort and support."

We can be of help, not only to those outside our families, but to those within them as well. Grace has discovered that since her husband's passing, she is very much needed in her grandchildren's lives. Grace has a special way about her — quite sophisticated, a little feisty, totally sincere. She was married to a bright, intelligent man named Oscar, who had received a Ph.D. in Religion and Philosophy from the University of Southern California in the mid-1940s.

Grace and Oscar worked closely together for a number of years in the ministry. Grace was blessed with a beautiful voice, which she shared on many

I sit with the man or woman who has just lost their spouse and I say, "If you want to cry, I'll cry with you. If you want to be quiet, I'll be quiet with you. When you want to talk, I'll listen." —RUTH

occasions. In their forty-eight years of marriage, Oscar taught at a number of universities across the United States. They traveled widely, holding teaching assignments and conducting retreats in South Africa, Swaziland, Australia, and the Philippines.

During their years of marriage, they were blessed with three children and several grandchildren, who have been Grace's main focus since her husband passed away from cancer in 1991. As Grace was grieving the loss of her partner, she thought of her grandchildren and how she could help shape these young lives while still in their formative years. With this goal in mind and a desire to be near her children, she decided to move to the Los Angeles area.

Grace lives by the scriptures found in the Old Testament book of Ecclesiastes (3:1 NIV): "There is a time for everything, and a season for every activity under heaven." Another of Grace's favorite scriptures is also found in Ecclesiastes (3:11 NIV): "He has made everything beautiful in its time! He has also set eternity in the hearts of men; yet they cannot fathom what God has done from beginning to end." Grace is finding great joy and fulfillment in her life because she continues to contribute to the lives of others.

REAWAKENINGS

↩ *Protect your need to grieve and rebuild your life.* We all need to pace ourselves, giving ourselves plenty of time to feel the full range of our emotions. Be on the lookout for the tendency to numb yourself to the pain through excessive activity, especially by losing yourself in the needs of others.

⤳ *As you heal, be open to helping others.* We all move forward in the context of relationships. If we isolate ourselves, not only do we stunt our own progress but we deprive others of what we have to offer. Work toward a balance of give and take.

⤳ *Recognize your unique gifts.* Now that you are in the process of rebuilding your life, you are equipped like never before to help others traveling a similar path. Don't sell yourself short. You have a lot to offer.

⤳ *Let God lead you.* On a daily basis God will help you be in the world in a new way, in a good way. Your new life will be built on the solid foundation of your past.

CHAPTER EIGHT

TIME FOR ROMANCE?

I've heard many women say they'll never remarry after their husbands pass away. But dismiss all previous thoughts of whether it is possible to love again. It is. And if it's right for you, God will lead the way.   —ANNETTE

"Are you going to remarry?" That's a question most of us are asked sooner or later in the process of re-building our lives. In order to answer that question, we must ask ourselves many more questions: Is it time yet for me to be thinking about being with another man? If I wanted to date, where would I meet a loving, appropriate man? How would my family, especially my children, react to a new man in my life? Do I even want to start over with someone new? Might life be easier to continue on my own?

The first time anyone mentioned the possibility that I might remarry, I was shocked. I still felt married to David, and the suggestion seemed almost obscene to me! I've spoken with other women who share this feeling, viewing their late husbands as their *only* husbands. While it may seem like this feeling would be common among older women who have lived many years with the same man, some younger women also find the idea of remarriage almost beyond comprehension. Having made a lifelong commitment to a particular man, it can be difficult to picture yourself with someone else.

Inez told me that she and her husband had joked about whether or not either of them would remarry if the other died. "We'd laughed about it because it seemed so far-fetched at the time. I'd say, 'If I go first, I know you'll be married in no time. And I just want you to know that I'm going to be sitting on the bedpost after I die and haunt your bedroom. I'll sit here and say, "Here I am, Chet. You behave yourself!" He'd laugh, 'That's exactly where I won't want you to be!'

"I think he would have remarried, even though I haven't. I told that story once at church and a woman we know said, 'That's right, I'd have been the first one in line if he was a widower.' I think most anybody would have felt lucky to have him for a husband."

But for Inez, there is no one else. Even though it's been many years since Chet passed away, Inez

---

Having made a lifelong commitment to a particular man, it can be difficult to picture yourself with someone else. —MARY ELLEN

---

still dreams about him. "In the dreams I have most often about Chet, we are not together. He's there. I'm here. No matter how I try, there's always this distance between us. There's a sadness to the dreams and a level of frustration at not being able to get to him."

Inez's expression turns from sadness to am impish smile. "I had one dream that was very vivid in which Chet was with another woman! I never knew who it was, but he was with her and kissing and carrying on. I was just furious in the dream! I can't tell you how furious I was. In fact, I woke up furious. I was furious all day long. It didn't matter that it was a dream. I have a large picture of him in the hallway, and I refused to look at it all day." Inez laughed at herself. "It's a wonder that I didn't throw it out the window!

"That dream let me know that I still feel connected to Chet, regardless of how many years it has been. I've been asked out by various men. Some were looking for friendship and some wanted something more romantic. But I decline any invitations other than group events. If I met someone I wanted to date, I would. But honestly, I still feel married to Chet."

STEPPING FORWARD OR SIDESTEPPING?

Timing is one of the major factors we face in deciding whether to love someone else romantically. Have you taken the time to genuinely grieve the loss of your husband? While the comfort of someone new can appeal to some women, I've learned through my interviews that having a new relationship does not necessarily make it easier to accept the death of your husband. Leslie was one of those women who moved ahead too quickly. She told me that she did not really embrace her grief for about two years after her husband's death. You might ask, "How could that be? How could she escape those terrible first painful, stressful moments? What about the loneliness?" Leslie unwittingly postponed her pain by trying to start a new life too soon.

She recalled, "My husband, Woody, left for work early in the morning, shortly after four-thirty. A large tractor-trailer collided with him, pinning his small truck underneath, where he was burned beyond recognition. They had to use his dental records to identify him.

"Our family is well-known in our denomination, so the news of Woody's death traveled around the world in a matter of hours. I received condolences from friends everywhere.

"Looking back now, the first weeks and months were such a blur. I just took care of our three children, aged thirteen months to ten years, and put one foot in front of the other."

Since Leslie had been a stay-at-home mom and had never planned to work outside the home, she was not prepared for this turn in her life. Through a settlement from her husband's accident and assistance from friends and family, she continued to stay home with her children and give them all her love and understanding.

Leslie told me, "I was so grateful for all the help I received, especially from Sam, one of Woody's friends. He was divorced and knew what it was like to be a single parent. My kids really liked him, and he began to spend more and more time with us. He did repairs around the house and became the person I relied on whenever there were things that I just couldn't manage. Within five months after Woody's accident, we were a couple.

"At first, I did not know how to deal with my feelings, or even what those feelings were. I met with my minister, who knew the entire situation very well. I was concerned about what other people would think. Was I doing the wrong thing in allowing this relationship to continue? My minister told me not to worry about what others might think but to do what I felt was best for my family."

For the next two years, Leslie and Sam continued their relationship, which felt like such a gift to her and her children. They often talked about marriage and the blending of his family with hers. In time, they became engaged, but only for a short time. The more Leslie and Sam talked about the future and all that was involved in joining two families, the more unsure Leslie became. "I wondered whether joining these two families would be good for my children and whether this marriage would serve the best interest of his children. More and more doubts arose, and the closer we came to setting a date, the more I felt reluctant to move forward.

"After a lot of prayer, discussion, and agonizing, I had clarity. I cared for Sam, but I was not in love with him. I was not reconciled to the fact that Woody was actually gone and that I was, indeed, a single woman. It felt like one moment I was married to Woody, then a blur, and then I was sitting next to Sam. I knew I had to end the relationship with Sam in order to grieve the loss of my husband.

"How right this decision was became clear when Sam walked out the door. I burst out in sobs, not because Sam was leaving, but because Woody was gone. My mourning was just beginning, and all the postponed grief emerged for the first time."

Perhaps the most difficult part of sorting through the past two years was acknowledging that, while she loved her children dearly, she had neglected

There were many times when I felt that I could not go on, and I wondered whether it would have been better if I'd married Sam. But deep in my heart I felt God telling me that my children and I needed to go through this experience, not try to sidestep it. —LESLIE

their feelings as much as her own. How could they grieve the loss of their father if she didn't? Leslie admitted, "Even though my children had asked many questions about the accident, as well as normal questions young children have about death, I realized that there was so much more we needed to talk about. I'd never intentionally neglected them and their needs, but I knew that for them to grow beyond this loss, I'd have to lead the way."

Leslie finally began to mourn her loss. She told me, "There were many times when I felt that I could not go on, and I wondered whether it would have been better if I'd married Sam. But deep in my heart I felt God telling me that my children and I needed to go through this experience, not try to sidestep it." Now, twenty years after the loss of her husband, tears come to her eyes as she recalls those precious moments of bonding with her children as they discussed their father's fatal accident. Years can't erase those painful moments, but she can smile through the tears.

"Today, I feel so grateful for the decision I made eighteen years ago. Jake, who was ten at the time of Woody's passing, is now a man. I'm so proud of him for the caring person he's become. He gave up a very lucrative job to help rebuild the homes and lives of those suffering in Kosovo. He knows how to help others rebuild because he went through that himself. Alison is now a wife and mother to two beautiful young children, and I'm a grandmother! And Grant, who was only thirteen months old when Woody died, will graduate from college in a few months. I couldn't be prouder of them or of the life we built for ourselves."

When asked whether she would ever remarry, Leslie considered. "I may remarry at some point, but finding a husband is not what my life's about. It's about living courageously with what comes into my life and trusting God to help me go through, not around, the difficulties."

Learning to accept the turns and twists in one's life, especially the unexpected and painful ones, is a theme I heard over and over in my interviews. For those women with children, abruptly becoming a single parent is challenging enough without all the other stresses of widowhood. As a single parent, taking our children's feelings into consideration can play a major part in our decision to remarry or to remain single. In the same way that Leslie placed a priority on her children's concerns, Marvis also considered how remarriage would impact her daughter after her husband's death.

Marvis and Lester met in their hometown of Carrington, North Dakota, and began dating. After a lengthy courtship, Marvis decided the slow pace of life in Carrington was not for her. She applied for and got a sixth-grade teaching position in Oxnard, California. After she left, Lester realized that he cared more for Marvis than he'd known. Not about to lose the girl of his dreams, Lester followed Marvis to California and resumed their courtship. They were married two years later, when Marvis was twenty-nine.

In the summer of 1953, Marvis and Lester had Debbie. Lester fell in love with his baby girl, and a strong bond formed between father and daughter. When Lester was fifty years old, doing well in his own business, he was diagnosed with cancer. Although the outlook was bleak from the beginning, Lester followed his doctor's orders religiously. He firmly believed the cure for cancer was just around the corner, and as he went through extensive treatment and discomfort, he clung to hopes that "the cure" would come soon. Every day was another precious gift to him and his family. In spite of everyone's efforts, Lester died at the age of fifty-one.

Marvis was now a widow with a ten-year-old to raise. They moved out of the family home into an apartment as a way to distance themselves from difficult memories. Marvis became the family's sole supporter, while tackling the changes that come with moving and being a single parent.

Marvis knew that she had to be strong for her daughter and for herself. "As much as I loved my husband, I was determined to make a new life for myself and my daughter." Being a young, attractive, bright, and energetic woman, Marvis was often pursued by male friends. "A few years after

Lester passed away, I started dating. But the thought of me being with anyone but her father upset my daughter greatly. Debbie was entering adolescence without the father she adored, and I decided that it would be better for both of us if she went through her teen years without another major adjustment. So I stopped going out and focused all my attention on my priorities — my daughter, my teaching, and my church.

"I never made the decision not to marry again. I was open to romance after Debbie was grown. But by the time that happened, my life was very comfortable. No one has come along who captured my heart as Lester once did. It's not that I planned to remain single. I just took one step at a time, a step that was right for me at that time, and this is where I ended up. I feel very good about the direction my life has taken."

WHEN THE TIME IS RIGHT

While children may play a part in their mothers' remaining single, children can also catalyze new romance. Several years after Margaret's husband died of cancer, Debbie, her daughter, and Al, her son-in-law, decided she would be a perfect match for Ed, a handsome widower who attended their church. They discussed their idea with Dick and Crystal, Ed's son and daughter-in-law, and the four "kids" put some effort into making a "magical match."

They launched their scheme by inviting both extended families for a weekend on a ranch that Margaret's daughter and son-in-law owned. While all the other family members were out having fun during the day, Ed stayed in nursing an injured foot. Margaret decided to keep him company. At the day's end, they were quite smitten with each other. While this budding relationship had begun in March 1990, it took a trip together to Europe a year later for it to reach full bloom. Ed was planning to join a tour group in Europe with friends the following July. With his children's encouragement, Ed suggested that Margaret consider joining the group. Their relationship grew on this trip. They experienced all the teenage awkwardness in the beginning. Margaret giggled, "As we traveled over the beautiful European countryside, seated next to each other on the bus, the very touch of the hairs on Ed's arm brushing my arm gave me a fantastic thrill of a new love."

There was a bitter sweetness to this trip for Margaret, however. Some years earlier, before Warren's illness and death, she and Warren had taken a wonderful trip to many of the same places. As Ed was holding Margaret in his arms in Paris, declaring his love for her, she began to cry. Ed understood. He was experiencing a bittersweet moment as well. You see, the original plan for this trip was made long ago before the passing of Ed's first wife, Donna. This was to have been "their trip." Through Ed's and Margaret's tears, they embraced a new beginning. They felt that this was a very special moment for them, ordained by God. So commenced a great second marriage for two wonderful people. They recently celebrated their ten-year anniversary with another marvelous trip.

New romance can take us by surprise. Annette told me, "After close to four decades of marriage to my husband, Gene, who had been a Navy fighter pilot, health and physical education teacher, coach, and administrator of physical education for a large city school system, it seemed almost unbelievable to learn that he had a malignant brain tumor."

The oncologist gave Gene twelve to eighteen months. The neurosurgeon said he had never seen anyone with Gene's condition live longer than two years. After the first surgery, Gene underwent chemotherapy, radiation, laetrile treatment, and vitamin therapy. Miraculously, Gene lived a relatively normal life for the next eight years. Annette believes "that God touched Gene and allowed him those extra years to love and enjoy his grandchildren and family. We were able to take two trips to Europe during this time, so I have those precious memories."

As we traveled over the beautiful European countryside, seated next to each other on the bus, the very touch of the hairs on Ed's arm brushing my arm gave me a fantastic thrill of a new love. —MARGARET

However, the malignant tumor returned, and the last nine months of Gene's life were very stressful for the family. Annette recalled, "We turned our family room into as cheerful a room as we possibly could, and Gene stayed at home until the day he died.

152

"I was in a daze after his death. I certainly had no interest in getting involved with anyone else. Instead, I spent time with my women friends. One dear friend asked whether I would enjoy traveling with her. Of course, it didn't take me long to say, 'I would love to. I need a rest.'

"We took a marathon trip by car through the South, on to Florida, up the East Coast, through Washington, D.C., Boston, and New England. It was springtime, and I felt new life coming back into my very being. The travel was very therapeutic for my tired body and aching heart."

After returning from her travels, Annette invested herself in the women's Bible study at her church, daily looking after her mother in a nearby nursing home, caring for her granddaughter after school, keeping house, and minding her rental properties.

With a twinkle in her eye, Annette declared, "I've heard many women say they'll never remarry after their husbands pass away. But dismiss all your thoughts of whether it is possible to love again. It is. And if it's right for you, God will lead the way."

"About two years after Gene passed away, I began to see a gentleman whom we had known along with his wife in our community and church. His wife died after a long illness a few years before my husband. Our friends and interests were very compatible. Most importantly, he made me laugh again.

"We were married in a private, simple ceremony. I never dreamed that I could have such a wonderful relationship after my marriage for so many years with Gene. I have found Coburn to be such a gentle, loving person. He compliments me often, which gives me a marvelous sense of security. He shows me so much appreciation for even the simplest meals that I prepare. I truly believe he was God's gift to me."

Is it time for romance? Only you can answer that question for yourself. None of us has to give a final answer to that question. Who knows who might be right around the corner?

REAWAKENINGS

↩ *Recognize that you don't need a man to be happy.*
While you may always miss your late husband, be open to living a full and meaningful life as a single woman. Some women are content on

their own, satisfied with memories of the love of their life.

⤳ *Don't jump into a new romance prematurely.* It's tempting to put off grieving by distracting yourself with another man. But sooner or later, the grief work must be done if you're to rebuild your life. Take time to feel and express your feelings. When the time is right, a new romance may become part of this new phase of life.

⤳ *Never say never.* You may think you're past the point of loving again, but you might just meet someone who is a perfect fit for this phase of your life. Be open to possibilities.

CHAPTER NINE

UNEXPECTED TREASURE
AND UNTAPPED TALENTS

A friend from church paid me a high compliment by saying, "You get more done by accident than most people do on purpose." When I look back, I think my most rewarding accomplishments were those I never intended to achieve. —ETHEL

Eileen and Bill's exciting plan for his retirement centered around a cabin they were building in California near Lake Tahoe. "As the house was being built, we dreamed of how my husband, a successful doctor, could get some relief from the stressful demands on his time. He wanted a cabin located on one of the golf courses. If Bill wasn't playing golf, he could sit and watch the other golfers. Bill had anticipated many happy hours there. I wanted a place where I could relax and enjoy the gorgeous surroundings, and where our three sons, their wives, and our ten grandchildren could enjoy the sports and activities. As we set out on the seven-hour drive to spend our first night in the cabin, Bill and I felt so very fortunate to have such a wonderful place.

"As we traveled toward Lake Tahoe, we caught glimpses of the beautiful blue lake framed by rich vegetation. The lake with all its surroundings is truly a breathtaking sight—the shimmering blue water, sandy beaches along the shore, green golf courses dotted with many small villages. Our dream had come true.

"We arrived, had dinner, and retired for our very first night in our dream place. I slept great. The next morning, I woke early to a sunny, blue-sky day. Unable to resist an early morning walk, I quietly got dressed and tiptoed out, not wanting to wake Bill from his much-needed sleep. After escaping the big city of Los Angeles, I could smell the wonderful fresh air. The birds were in great chorus that morning. Even the smell of the lush green grass was exhilarating. After I'd walked some distance, I thought it was time for me to return lest Bill awaken and find me gone.

"As I went into the bedroom to see whether Bill was awake, I noticed that he was in the exact same position as when I left him. I sensed something wrong, and as soon as I saw his face, I knew that sometime in the night he had passed away in his sleep. Amid the shock and disbelief, I began making phone calls to our sons and relatives. Here I was all alone, miles from home, and Bill gone. Help was on the way, but I couldn't stop crying. And I couldn't stay alone in the cabin; I couldn't stand to see Bill in this condition.

"Our cabin was located on one of the golf courses, so I walked over and sat down on a very large rock, sobbing, my mind a large vacuum. I looked up to see three golfers. One golfer teed off, and through my daze it seemed to me that the ball was heading in my direction. The eyes of the three golfers were also following the ball as it sailed high in the sky. As it began its downward descent, I felt sure that the ball was going to hit me. I prayed, 'Lord, are Bill and I going to die on the same day?'

"The ball hit the ground a few feet away, and I went back to crying over Bill. Quickly the golfers came running toward me, thinking I was crying out in pain. Between sobs I assured them that the ball had not hit me, but that I was waiting for the coroner because my husband had died in his sleep, and I did not want to be at the cabin when his body was removed. They were both relieved that I was physically okay, yet very sympathetic to my distress."

Eileen and her husband had looked forward to many leisurely days together in their cabin hide-away. No one expected their first night in the cabin to be Bill's last day on earth. Eileen's life had taken a wrenching turn. She recalled, "I had driven up that mountain with my husband and our joyous expectations. But I hardly remember the ride back down. I felt like I was freefalling into a dark abyss."

Bill died at the age of sixty-five, after he and Eileen had been married forty-two years. One of his most treasured volunteer efforts was serving as chairman of the board of trustees for a university. He placed a high priority on education, and the hours he spent on campus with the students were some of his happiest. Eileen told me, "Before Bill died, we discussed how he might contribute more to the university, but we didn't make any definite plans. After all, Bill was only in his 'early years.'

We thought there would be plenty of time to make those kinds of decisions."

After Bill's sudden passing, Eileen confronted the many tasks all widows must face. In the back of her mind, she felt that someday she would follow through on Bill's dream to help students in some way. Eventually, she and her sons established a memorial in his honor—The William Little Memorial Scholarship Fund. Eileen explained, "We decided to award four-year scholarships to needy students with a strong desire to achieve academically. The interest from this fund gives a bright young student the opportunity to pursue an education at the same institution where Bill had devoted so much of his time and energy. At that point in my life, I was still focused totally on Bill's dreams, unaware that God was going to use this opportunity for my benefit as well.

"I never dreamed that it would be so rewarding personally to help someone to further his or her education. Our first student was highly recommended to us by some of her professors. Hilda was going to have to drop out at the end of her first quarter because she lacked the funds to continue. My sons and I set high standards for the scholarship—a

3.8 grade point average and serious financial need. Hilda qualified on both counts. We supported her for four years, and she spoke four languages by the time she graduated. Hilda then spent a year in Germany as an intern in a branch of the government.

It's so exciting to invest in the lives of these young people and know that I've made a difference that will last long beyond my husband's or my life span.
— EILEEN

She earned her master's degree and is presently teaching at a college in northern California.

"Our second scholarship student is the son of a missionary. After graduating with high honors, Ronnie assisted in medical labs for two years. He then earned his master's degree at UCLA in physical ecology. He is presently a project manager in one of the largest biotech companies in the world."

What started as a way for Eileen to honor her late husband and to cope with her grief has become for her an unexpected source of vitality and a sense of the future. "It's so exciting to invest in the lives of these young people and know that I've made a difference that will last long beyond my husband's or my life span. My 'family' is expanding each time we sponsor another student. We are now eagerly awaiting our sixth student. This one is interested in medicine. It is interesting to see the different areas each one is pursuing." By losing herself in this tribute to her husband, she has found a new calling for her own life.

HIS MISSION BECAME MY MISSION

Eileen isn't the only woman to be surprised by unexpected treasures found in a new calling. Jonnie fulfilled her husband's lifelong desire to contribute to missions after Clyde passed away from cancer at the age of seventy-eight. Jonnie recalled, "Clyde's family and my family had farms next to each other in Oklahoma. Our families were very close, always helping each other out. Some of my earliest memories of Clyde were when I was only thirteen and he was a young man of eighteen. His sister was my best friend.

"When I was fourteen, my family sold the farm in Oklahoma and moved to northern California.

Around that time, World War II broke out and Clyde joined the Air Force as a pilot. After some time, a long-distance romance blossomed, and when the war ended in 1945, we were married."

After the first few years of marriage and the birth of their daughter, Janet, Clyde decided he wanted to go into medicine, with the vision of possibly becoming a medical missionary. He enrolled in college at the age of twenty-nine. He graduated with his bachelor's degree in three and a half years and was accepted into Loma Linda Medical School. By the time Clyde finished his schooling and was ready to practice medicine as an anesthesiologist, he was thirty-nine years old, and Janice, their only daughter, was in high school. Jonnie and Clyde reluctantly decided that the time to go into missionary work had passed.

Meanwhile, Jonnie received LVN training and was instrumental in setting up Clyde's medical practice in southern California. Clyde practiced in several of the local hospitals, and eventually he and several colleagues established the Arcadia Outpatient Hospital. Clyde never lost his interest in medical missions, and he was able to fulfill some of his dreams by helping train some of the missionaries in anesthesiology when they returned home on furlough.

Clyde truly loved his work, and he retired in 1992 after thirty-two years of full-time practice. Clyde also loved life, and when it was discovered that he was suffering from cancer, the entire family entered into a valiant fight against the disease. The best treatment available was sought, with no stone left unturned for finding a cure. Jonnie sums up their life with these fitting and beautiful thoughts: "If it was destined that our book of life would end, I would want to say that we found the last chapter very rich with new interests and energy for sharing our joys, our faith, and even our concerns in a new intimate way. We discovered gems of our personality we hadn't known before. If I gleaned one dominant memory of our last chapter, it was that of our enduring love, no matter what.

"After Clyde died, I wanted to do something in honor of his love for missions and medicine. Our church denomination has a hospital in Washim, India, the Reynolds Memorial Hospital. Clyde loved children, and he was interested in giving the many helpless babies born in Africa a better chance of life. So in my husband's memory,

I made a contribution to the hospital's pediatrics ward. Knowing that his life is memorialized in this way gives me enormous comfort."

Following through on dreams once held by your husband may serve as a gratifying way to build a new phase of life on the solid foundation of your past. Betty found this to be true after her husband, William, passed away from cancer. William, born in East Prussia, had immigrated to the United States when he was nineteen. While studying in New York, he became interested in linguistics. After researching different countries in Central America, he learned that there were more than twenty tribes in that area whose culture and customs had not changed significantly since they were discovered by the early Spanish explorers.

When Betty was a young girl, a missionary from Guatemala, Miss Philips, lived with her family for a year. Miss Philips told her many stories about Guatemala, and Betty wondered whether she might want to be a missionary herself. After she graduated from college, Betty received an invitation from Miss Philips to teach music and languages in Guatemala, where William and Betty met.

After Betty completed her year of teaching, she returned to the United States. In spite of the geographical distance, their courtship flourished. After three years, William proposed marriage, and Betty returned to Guatemala, where she and William lived and raised a family. William served as a Bible translator and worked diligently on his linguistic translations. In 1961, he was honored for translating the entire New Testament into the Kekchi language. This tribe, of approximately three hundred thousand people, is related to the great Mayans.

Betty explained, "After William finished the Kekchi translation, he was asked to start work on translating the New Testament for the Pokomchi Indians. In 1970, shortly before we left for a one-year furlough to the United States, William translated the first eight books of the New Testament into Pokomchi. We went back to the States fully expecting to return and finish the project.

"On the trip back to Guatemala from the United States, William started driving erratically and complained of painful headaches. It got so bad that I took over driving and finished our journey.

"As soon as we arrived home, I took William to the hospital. They ordered a brain scan, and the news was very bleak. Our worst fears were realized when the doctors told us that William had an inoperable brain tumor. Chemotherapy could extend his life a few months, but it offered no hope for recovery. Furthermore, the doctor advised that we fly back to the United States immediately."

William did not want to live his last days suffering the side effects of treatment, so he and Betty decided to fly to San Francisco, where he could be close to three of their four children. Betty recalled, "I don't know what I would have done without my children and without the time we all had together before William passed away. It was certainly hard on all of us, but we also had the opportunity to truly treasure our lives together." Just three short months after his initial diagnosis, William died, but not before he shared precious moments with his family, memories that still help soothe the pain.

After he died, Betty didn't feel at home in the States. She longed to return to Guatemala and finish the translation that William had started. Something called her to fulfill the dream so close to

William's heart. As wonderful as it was to have her children nearby, she could not escape that small voice deep within her. Her prayer had been, from the time of William's death, for knowledge of God's intentions for her future. She could not forget the place she had spent the last thirty-one years with William. And yet she wondered whether she could manage on her own. Could she cope with returning without her husband? Would it be possible for her to pick up where he had left off?

Less than a year after William had passed away, Betty was welcomed back by all the friends she and her husband had left behind in Guatemala. Even though Betty did not have her husband's linguistic or theological education, she had studied Pokomchi and had learned the methods of research and translation by observing William over the years. Enthusiastically, she dove into the unfinished translation.

Betty remained in Guatemala for the next eleven years directing the team, of translators that completed the task of giving the Pokomchi Indians the New Testament in their language. She said, "If you include the time William put into this work, it took us seventeen years to fully translate the

New Testament." The work was finally dedicated in July 1983.

Betty's life work is interwoven with William's. On the surface, it may have looked like William was the one doing the important work, with Betty dismissible as a mere missionary's wife. Before William's passing, Betty had invested her talents in raising her children. Afterward, however, she found her own life's calling by seeing William's vision through to the end.

NEW OPPORTUNITIES

We don't need to go to some exotic location to discover our untapped talents or uncover unexpected treasures. We all have opportunities to explore new endeavors. Mary, the mother of eleven children, found a new vision for her life after Joseph, her husband, died very unexpectedly.

Mary told me, "Since my husband was a physician, he was away from home a lot, and I learned to manage a very busy household on my own. Not only did I have eleven children to raise, my youngest son was born disabled. I ran everything singlehandedly. Whatever needed to be fixed or repaired, I either fixed it myself or knew who to call."

Mary had a very independent spirit, something she admits Joseph did not always appreciate. "By the time the children were getting older and leaving home, I began to enjoy having some time for myself. My husband was a good father and provided very well for the family, but he was also full of ideas about how I should spend my time. He urged me to research legal issues related to disability, even though I had not the slightest interest in law. Joseph was strong willed and difficult when crossed at times."

When her husband passed away, Mary was sixty-five and still full of life and vision. Immediately, she returned to social work, the career she had chosen before she had her first child. "I went back to school and got my license as a clinical social worker. I have found my niche. Since my last son is disabled, I specialize in either helping parents with disabled children or children with disabled parents. My son was fifteen years old at the time of his father's death. Even though he is now twenty-eight years old, he will always need care." She knows firsthand about the many difficult situations for disabled people. She is able to advocate for her son and for the many other disabled people in her community.

"To be honest," Mary confided, "I felt controlled by my husband during our marriage. He was definitely in charge. I loved him and, at times, sorely miss his companionship. But it is wonderful to make my own decisions." At seventy-eight, Mary is a bundle of energy with great love and heart for her work. She's very convincing when she glows, "I love my life!"

ON THE ROAD AGAIN

Along with Mary, I also feel I enjoy life in ways I never expected. My husband and I shared a special love for the Japanese people since 1975, when David taught in Japan for the University of Southern California in the Graduate Program Abroad. We later returned to Japan in 1985, where we taught in a junior college sponsored by our church denomination until 1989.

One afternoon in Japan, while David was taking the train home from class, he saw a young Japanese woman enter the train. He stood up and offered her his seat, and she said "Thank you!" He asked her if she spoke English, which she did. In fact, she owned and operated her own English academy. She introduced herself as Sumiyo, and they exchanged phone numbers. This was the beginning of what we consider a God-ordained friendship.

Sumiyo and her husband, Sanji, have since become our dearest friends, like family. In fact, when

To be honest, I felt controlled by my husband during our marriage. He was definitely in charge. I loved him and, at times, I sorely miss his companionship. But it is wonderful to make my own decisions. —MARY

David had his accident, Sumiyo flew in from Tokyo to help me and Carmen with his care. Sanji joined her later, and they were both able to spend time with David before he passed away.

Sumiyo now runs an antique import business and has partnered with me as I have developed my own small company. I purchase antique lace, usually from the Victorian era, and create a variety of products, such as aprons, dresses, doll clothes, tea cozies, and fancy lampshades. I ship these items to Sumiyo's shop, where she sells them to her many customers. I have traveled to Japan since David's passing to visit Sumiyo and Sanji, to help with her classes, and to simply enjoy their company. Sometimes I travel alone, but it is wonderful when Carmen or my close friend Judy Berry (no relation) accompany me. The Japanese fell in love with Judy when she shared her wonderful talent on the violin.

One of the challenges of traveling is finding someone to go with us — someone with whom we are compatible. After years of marriage, you and your husband have had time to work out your idiosyncrasies around the snoring, the night trips to the bathroom, and the need to get up early or sleep late. But it's worth the effort of finding someone who will enjoy traveling with you. As Inez told me, "At first I thought I'd have to give up traveling after my husband died because you can't travel with just anybody, especially if you share a room. I'm a restless sleeper and am up and down all night, making noise. I convinced my friend Elena to go with me, and she turned out to be a great companion. She is deaf in one ear, and I don't bother her because she sleeps on her good ear."

Many of the women I spoke with found great healing in "getting away from it all." It can be very important for us to prove to ourselves that we can still find alternative ways to pursue our love for

At first I thought I'd have to give up traveling after my husband died because you can't travel with just anybody, especially if you share a room. I'm a restless sleeper and am up and down all night, making noise. I convinced my friend Elena to go with me, and she turned out to be a great companion. She is deaf in one ear, and I don't bother her because she sleeps on her good ear.
—INEZ

adventure. Ethel bragged, "I drive to Myrtle Beach, South Carolina, every winter and meet my brother, his wife, and some Canadian snowbird friends. I have for the last five years since Harold died.

"At first, I thought I absolutely needed a travel companion, so I asked a friend to go with me. She sprained her ankle the first night out so she couldn't help me drive a bit. I found out then that I could drive the entire distance myself. The next year I took my minister's wife just for the fun of it.

We weren't half an hour from home before she became sick. So the next two years I drove by myself. I have motels booked, and I know exactly where I'm going to be. But it was a challenge for me to do something by myself. I've gained so much self-confidence!"

When we reflect on the time we shared with our husbands, we'll find ourselves with fewer regrets if we help ourselves experience comfort now. Even if there are things that we would do differently if given the chance, it's possible through God's grace to make peace with these feelings. In my interviews, I've realized that those women who live in the present with passion and enthusiasm have the fewest regrets. They didn't hold back when their husbands were by their sides. This same stamina served them well when they confronted life without the men they loved.

"No regrets, I have absolutely no regrets." These were the words Gloria spoke in reflecting on the death of her husband, Frank, two years before. "We had recently celebrated our fiftieth wedding anniversary. Unlike some couples, we had not waited until retirement to begin to live.

"Both of us had been intensively involved in our separate careers, but we did not allow that to control our lives. We loved to travel and tried to put aside funds for a couple of trips each year. Frank added so much to my life, and we had so many common interests. In fact, we just enjoyed being with each other whether at home or abroad."

Gloria and Frank first met when she was four years old and he was fourteen. Gloria's parents and

---

I have no regrets. I wouldn't have done anything differently. There's great comfort in knowing that.

—GLORIA

Frank's parents attended the same church in Detroit. As Gloria grew up, Frank often visited in her home. At the early age of four, Gloria remembers how fond Frank was of her parents. Gloria smiled in recalling, "He had many girlfriends over the years. Girls were drawn to him like bees to honey. Frank went into the service during World War II, and during that time I grew up. After the war ended, Frank returned home. I was no longer the little girl he'd left behind. It wasn't long until we were dating, engaged, and married. The ten-year difference in our ages seemed insignificant to us. We were in love. I went from my mother's arms to Frank's arms."

In the 1950s, Frank's work brought him to Pasadena. They found a wonderful church and became very active in many ministries. Their first child, Janice, was born, and they thought they were well on their way to having the perfect family of six. In their daughter's early childhood, however, she developed brittle diabetes. Her medical care was so demanding that they felt it best to limit their family.

The years seemed to pass almost too quickly. Gloria was busy working on her doctorate at USC and later became the chairman of the education department at California State University, Los Angeles. Frank was involved in the automotive business. Retirement came, and they embraced it with open arms. They were even more able now to indulge in their passion for travel. They loved to learn of different cultures and meet different people.

In the spring of 1997, Frank sensed that he had a physical problem. The result was a double colostomy. That did not stop the travels. Gloria became an expert in assisting Frank with his special needs. Some people may have become homebound with this type of medical condition, but Frank and Gloria decided to keep enjoying their love for travel and their love for each other.

Gloria recounted, "One Tuesday morning, about two years after Frank's surgery, Frank and I had an early breakfast. We were preparing to leave for our separate Bible studies. Frank wanted to take a short rest before we left, and I assured him that I would wake him up in time. When I went in to awaken Frank, I immediately knew that something was wrong. I called the paramedics who responded quickly, but in spite of their efforts, Frank passed away.

"We knew that he had a serious illness, but his death came so quickly and unexpectedly. I've been especially blessed by two wonderful gifts in dealing with the pain of losing Frank. First, I experienced a feeling of such perfect peace after his passing that I know it had to come from God. Second, we lived life so fully that I have no regrets. I wouldn't have done anything differently. There's great comfort in knowing that." Gloria continues her travels, although no longer with Frank at her side. She has many friends who share her passion for adventure. Gloria has learned the secret of living life in the moment.

REAWAKENING/

‿ *Do something that honors your late husband.* Whether you personally underwrite or gather donations, a memorial fund can be a service in several ways. First, it keeps your husband's memory alive in the hearts and minds of those who knew him. Whatever his interests may have been, your efforts will extend his positive impact beyond his years on earth. Second, people will be helped by your efforts. You may provide scholarships to college, aid the homeless, promote child-abuse prevention, or support vital ministries at your church. Third, you'll find new purpose. You may start out motivated by love for your husband, but before you know it, you'll be engaged in meaningful work and contributing in ways you never imagined.

↶ *Follow in your late husband's footsteps.* (This may apply to only a few widows.) Some women find their calling by continuing the work their husbands began. You may be more familiar with your husband's work than anyone else and can step right into his shoes.

↶ *Find your own niche.* Many of us have put dreams and aspirations on hold in order to raise our families or to deal with other limitations in our marriages. Now is the time to blow the dust off those dreams and breathe new life into them. You have the opportunity to do all those things you always wanted to do.

↶ *Get on the road again.* Rather than feel housebound because you've lost your traveling partner, find a friend and get back on the road. Travel is one of the most rejuvenating and inspirational things we can do, so don't count yourself out. As safety permits, you may discover you prefer to travel solo, enjoying the solitude and the flexibility of making all your own decisions.

↶ *Release regrets and embrace gratitude.* Wishing things had been different won't change the past. Living in regret will, however, rob you of satisfaction you could have in the moment and blind you to the many wonderful ways that God is working in your life. Through eyes of gratitude, we see God's hand in our lives. While none of us will ever be glad that our husbands have passed away, we can nevertheless be grateful for how God has helped us through this difficult loss. Offer to God any regrets you may have and make way for gratitude for what you shared with your husband in your marriage.

CHAPTER TEN

THE OTHER SIDE OF GRIEF

As I write this last chapter, I'm reminded that it's
been nearly four years since my husband's accident
and death. Four years! It seems like yesterday and,
at the same time, like decades in the past. Some
mornings I wake up expecting to find him snooz-
ing in the bed beside me as he did for forty-six
years. Other days I'm so engaged in my many satisfying activities that it feels like I've been on my
own forever.

Life as I know it today suits me well. I live in
a beautiful condo just the right size — big enough
to accommodate my love of entertaining and my
various business endeavors, yet small enough for
me to maintain easily. After David passed away, I
moved closer to my church and to many friends,
so my social life is full and my spiritual needs are
nurtured. My daughter lives two blocks away and

checks in on me daily, making me feel safe and yet free to live my own life. My two cats, Sailor and Sadie, grace me with their presence and remind me regularly that I should feel honored to feed and pet them. A garden that keeps me active and rewards my efforts with beauty sits outside my front door. I can honestly say I am happy—happy in a different way than I was when my husband was alive, but happy nevertheless. And I'm grateful to still be a part of God's plan.

As my life demonstrates, as do the lives of the other women in this book, the loss of your husband can be faced with God's gracious love along with support from friends and family. At times it feels like the pain will never stop, but it does and it will. And then you'll actually enjoy, not merely endure, this new phase of living.

You'll know you're on the other side when. . . .

✎ *Memories bring more comfort than pain.*

When we first begin this journey, memories of our husbands grip our hearts with pain. As we stumble in slow, uneven steps to "the other side," those same memories provide unexpected comfort. What my husband and I shared together comprise some of the best experiences of my life. What a shame it would be if for the rest of my life recalling those warm, funny, and even ridiculous experiences only triggered tears. Fortunately God has created us in such a way that many of the painful recollections fade, leaving colorful images for humorous retelling.

No one but you knows which painful moments may trigger that instant flood of tears. I am certain, however, that a particular memory can be transformed from a source of pain to a soothing reminder of shared love. My daughter gave David and me two mugs one Christmas. One had been inscribed Fabulous Father and the other read Magnificent Mother. These little gifts became integral to our morning ritual of sharing a cup of tea.

During David's hospitalization, I didn't give the mugs a second thought, but months after his death, as I packed up to leave our home, I didn't know what to do with the Fabulous Father mug. On one hand, it hurt too much to see that mug in my kitchen cabinet, but I couldn't just throw it away. I hid it away behind my other mugs where I couldn't see it. I couldn't even think of actually using it.

The other day, I took the Fabulous Father mug from the shelf and held it in my hands. A smile came to my face as I remembered some of the conversations David and I had shared while we sipped our tea. I decided to brew up a pot of tea and soon was lost in fond memories as I sipped from David's mug. I found that simple act healing and enjoyable. I'll keep his mug because it is a part of my past that I want to remember. David may not be here to share a morning brew, but his mug is here, and it comforts me.

Your memories will differ, but the process will be the same. You may have had a favorite restaurant, and for a long time, you didn't even want to drive by it, let alone eat there. Or maybe he bought you a special dress that you've hidden in the back of your closet. Wearing it again has seemed impossible. Perhaps you took a trip not long before he passed away, and looking at that photo album has been too painful. Eventually, you'll savor the food along with the memories at that particular restaurant, you'll proudly wear his favorite dress, and those pictures of the two of you having such a wonderful time together will remind you that your lives together were spent well. The time will surely come when those memories bring more comfort than pain.

~ *You focus more on the present than your past.*

This moment is all any of us has. It may be tempting to numb ourselves to this reality, but in fact a life well lived is one lived in present time — not in the past or future tense. We are privileged at this time in our lives to greet a new way of being in the world. In the book of Proverbs, Solomon reminds us that "a cheerful heart is good medicine, but a crushed spirit dries up the bones" (Proverbs 17:22 NIV), and that the wisdom found in God's words is "life to those who find them and health to a man's whole body" (Proverbs 4:22 NIV).

It is important to give yourself permission to be happy here and now. At first I felt guilty about laughing at a joke or enjoying a movie. I'd think, "How can you have a good time without David here?" Our husbands' memories are not honored by our living in the past, nor can God do his work through us. Enjoy this moment.

I also encourage you to take good care of your body and your spirit. Take time out for yourself.

Continue to let yourself heal. As women of faith, we can rely on the promises of our Heavenly Father, and we will find the spiritual, physical, and emotional healing we need. God still has a plan for our lives. Let's join with the psalmist, David, who said, "I wait for the Lord, my soul waits, and in his word I put my hope" (Psalms 130:5 NIV). Hope in your heart puts a smile on your face

↪ *You accept your new identity.*

At first I could not imagine living without my husband. Now, a few years later, I am comfortable as a single woman. My identity is no longer based on whom I am married to, although the man I *was* married to contributes greatly to the woman I am today. But I am more than my marital status. The fact that I have successfully coped with the loss of my husband has informed me that I'm a lot stronger and more resilient than I thought I was. I have sold and bought property, started my own business, landed a publishing contract, and planted the most beautiful roses in my garden. It is in this garden that my cat Sadie and I enjoy having breakfast. This is the place where I communicate with my Heavenly Father. I can think of no better way to begin my day than to thank God from the bottom of my heart for his faithfulness and his love shown to me each day. As I think of my tasks for the day and revel in God's goodness in my rose garden, I often sing these words:

IN THE GARDEN

I come to the garden alone while the dew is
    still on the roses.
And the voice I hear, falling in my ear, the Son
    of God discloses.
And he walks with me and he talks with me.
And, he tells me I am his own, and the joys
    we share
As we tarry there, none other has ever known.

No doubt you have other hymns or scriptures that anchor your identity firmly to God's heart. Singing or meditating on these words helps us see ourselves as God sees us, far beyond the grief that we've recently suffered.

↜ *You look forward to God's new plan for your life.*

My husband and I were a team, especially during the last decade of our marriage when we served as missionaries in Japan. When we returned to the States, the relationships we started with Japanese students continued, and David and I welcomed dozens of students into our home. They were touched deeply by David's life and his fatherly love for them. Without David beside me, I wondered whether our Japanese "daughters" would forget me and just what my role in their lives might be.

I didn't have to wait long for the answer. To my delight, the Japanese students I'd come to love visited and called me on a regular basis. I am always amazed when I receive a telephone call and I hear a familiar voice asking, "Is it okay if we come to visit you?" As their "American mother" I help them make career choices and discuss spiritual issues. I have even helped plan a wedding or two. This is just one of the ways God has reminded me that there is much left for me to do. The sense of God's presence is stronger than ever, and I know that, with divine assistance, wonderful adventures are in my future. We can rejoice with David when we read Psalms 139:16 NIV: "All the days ordained for me were written in your book before one of them came to be."

I want to welcome you to the other side of grief, where the sun sends rainbows into your life. You are not alone. In God's presence, I, along with many other women like me, am walking the same challenging, rewarding path. Whenever you're tempted to pull away from life, review these reawakenings and come back to all that God has for you.

THANK YOU, LORD!

Thank you, Lord, for daily strength:
Your loving kindness is a spring of joy.

You do not leave your beloved ones
Forsaken or alone:
You clothe them with goodness

In gentleness you lead them
Beside quiet waters,
Bathing their wounds.

O rejoice, all who listen!
Your God lives
And walks beside you
To comfort and renew.

Lord, you are my strength now!
Your incredible grace
So faithfully given
Fills me with joy.

Thank you for new hope;
You are within me and I rejoice!

—ESTHER REMINGTON

REAWAKENINGS

- ↪ Give yourself plenty of time to grieve.

- ↪ Put one foot in front of the other, one step at a time, and one day at a time.

- ↪ Expect good things.

- ↪ It's okay to be angry with God, or to be confused or unsure of your faith.

- ↪ Protect yourself from others who can't tolerate your feelings and doubts.

- ↪ Live in your faith and visit your doubts.

- ↪ Allow God's presence to comfort you.

- ↪ Hold on to the belief that God has a purpose for you.

- ↪ Work toward accepting that your life has changed and will never be the same.

- ↪ Don't expect to be perfect through this process.

- ↪ Don't push yourself.

- ↪ Model how to rebuild a life for your children.

- ↪ Keep fond memories of your husband alive.

- ↪ Make it okay to be happy.

- Accept support from your children.
- Transform traditions.
- Take comfort in memories.
- Don't waste time with "what ifs" when it comes to money.
- Become a financial student.
- Think creatively about your finances.
- Give yourself time to decide where to live.
- Be open to creative living arrangements.
- Let the process of going through your husband's belongings help you heal.
- Only keep what you want.
- Enjoy making your own decorating decisions.
- Protect your need to grieve and rebuild your life.
- As you heal, be open to helping others.
- Recognize your unique gifts.
- Let God lead you.
- Recognize that you don't need a man to be happy.
- Don't jump into a new romance prematurely.

- Never say never.
- Do something that honors your late husband.
- Follow in your late husband's footsteps.
- Find your own niche.
- Get on the road again.
- Release regrets and embrace gratitude.

About the Authors

MARY ELLEN BERRY, a business owner and retired middle school teacher, lost her husband of forty-six years in the winter of 1998 after a four-month hospitalization. Mary Ellen has confronted many of the issues associated with the loss of a spouse, including the selling of the family home, moving residences, coping with a changed financial situation, and redefining her life purpose. After two years of grieving, she had a transforming spiritual experience in which she discovered that she could enjoy life to its fullest measure.

Mary Ellen and her husband, David Berry, traveled extensively in Europe and Asia during their years together, including a four-year term teaching at a junior college near Tokyo, Japan. Since her husband's death, Mary Ellen has started her own design and textile importing business called Elegance by Ellen through which she designs and creates gift items sold exclusively through a Japanese specialty shop near Tokyo. She resides in Sierra Madre, California.

CARMEN RENEE BERRY has written and/or co-authored fifteen books including *girlfriends,* which was on the *New York Times* bestseller list for fifty-two weeks. Her accomplishments as an author have been featured in *People* magazine and *Newsweek,* and her articles have appeared in numerous national and professional publications. Carmen has appeared on hundreds of television and radio shows, including Oprah, Montel, Sally, The Early Show, and CNN. She has two master's degrees — one in Social Sciences from Northern Arizona University and one in Social Work from the University of Southern California. She resides in Sierra Madre, California.

OF RELATED INTEREST

Kim Jocelyn Dickson
GIFTS FROM THE SPIRIT
*Reflections on the Diaries and Letters
of Anne Morrow Lindbergh*

In *Gifts from the Spirit,* Dickson tells how her
own life has been transformed by Anne Morrow
Lindbergh's writings. Drawing from Lindbergh's
diaries, and including her own evocative reflections, Dickson captures the essence of Lindbergh's
spirituality and womanhood.

0-8245-2010-6, $17.95 hardcover

Brennan Manning
THE JOURNEY OF THE PRODIGAL
A Parable of Growth and Redemption

In *The Boy Who Cried Abba,* Brennan Manning
introduced readers to Willie Juan — an orphaned
boy who meets Jesus and learns the value of unconditional love. In this sequel, Willie Juan has
become an adult and, as he struggles with alco-
holism and depression, discovers that he has to
relearn the lessons of his childhood. His story is a
modern parable for our own search for wholeness
and unconditional love.

0-8245-2014-9, $14.95 paperback

crossroad

OF RELATED INTEREST

Paula D'Arcy
A NEW SET OF EYES
Encountering the Hidden God

Through a series of meditations and parables, D'Arcy helps readers awaken the mind to the presence of God, free the soul from its cherished idols, and infuse the emotions with joy. By the popular author of *Gift of the Red Bird* and *Song for Sarah*.

0-8245-1930-2, $16.95 hardcover

Michael L. Lindvall
THE GOOD NEWS FROM NORTH HAVEN
A Year in the Life of a Small Town

"A debut collection of...sermon-like tales covering a year in the life of a Presbyterian minister in a small Minnesota town — by a native of Minneapolis. Alter-ego Reverend David Battles arrived in the tiny town of North Haven fresh from seminary school and on his way to grander pulpits, but he and his family have discovered in their four years of small-town life that instead of outgrowing this backwater they've become attached to its every quirk and comfort — and have themselves become a local institution along the way."

—Kirkus

0-8245-2012-2, $16.95 paperback

crossroad

OF RELATED INTEREST

Barbara Fiand
IN THE STILLNESS YOU WILL KNOW
Exploring the Paths of Our Ancient Belonging

Popular spirituality writer Barbara Fiand is back with a moving book inspired by the death of her dearest friend and soulmate. Shadowed by grief, Fiand uses her friend's untimely passing as the starting point for ponderings about the nature of hope and the solace that comes from the beauty of nature speaking to us.

0-8245-2650-3, $16.95 paperback

Michael Morwood
GOD IS NEAR
Trusting Our Faith

In his latest book, the author of *Tomorrow's Catholic* and *Is God Jesus God?* reminds readers that the Christian God is closer to us than our very hearts. He seeks to counter commonly held notions — like the need for people to earn or be worthy of God's love — with the loving portrait of the Father handed down by Jesus and captured in the Gospels.

0-8245-1984-1, $12.95 paperback

crossroad

OF RELATED INTEREST BY
HENRI J. M. NOUWEN

THE HEART OF HENRI NOUWEN
Selected Readings

To commemorate the seventieth anniversary of Henri Nouwen's birth, Crossroad is issuing this anthology of the best of Henri Nouwen from our holdings. The volume focuses on the three themes that were closest to Henri's heart: hope in suffering, a personal relationship with God, and living for others.

0-8245-1985-X, $18.95 hardcover

Please support your local bookstore,
or call 1-800-707-0670 for Customer Service.

For a free catalog, write us at

THE CROSSROAD PUBLISHING COMPANY
481 Eighth Avenue, Suite 1550
New York, NY 10001

Visit our website at
www.crossroadpublishing.com

crossroad